2x4
OUTDOOR
PROJECTS

EASY DO-IT-YOURSELF PROJECTS

USING BASIC TOOLS

AND STANDARD LUMBER

THE FAMILY Handyman | The Family Handyman
Eagan, Minnesota

5

THE FAMILY Handyman
2x4
OUTDOOR PROJECTS

Editorial and Production Team

Vern Johnson, Peggy McDermott, Rick Muscoplat, Marcia Roepke, Mary Schwender

Photography and Illustrations

Ron Chamberlain, Tom Fenenga, Bruce Kieffer, Mike Krivit, Don Mannes, Ramon Moreno, Shawn Nielsen, Doug Oudekerk, Frank Rohrbach III, Eugene Thompson, Bill Zuehlke

Text, photography and illustrations for *2×4 Outdoor Projects* are based on articles previously published in *The Family Handyman* magazine (2915 Commers Dr., Suite 700, Eagan, MN 55121, familyhandyman.com). For information on advertising in *The Family Handyman* magazine, call (646) 293-6150.

ISBN: 978-1-62145-310-9

The Family Handyman

Editor in Chief   Gary Wentz
Project Editor   Eric Smith
Design & Layout   Diana Boger, Teresa Marrone
Project Manager   Mary Flanagan
Senior Editor   Travis Larson
Associate Editors   Jeff Gorton, Mark Petersen, Jason White
Office Administrative Manager   Alice Garrett
Set Builder   Josh Risberg
Senior Copy Editor   Donna Bierbach
VP, Group Publisher   Russell S. Ellis

Published by Home Service Publications, Inc., a subsidiary of Trusted Media Brands, Inc.

PRINTED IN CHINA

10 9 8 7 6 5 4 3 2 1

A Note to Our Readers

All do-it-yourself activities involve a degree of risk. Skills, materials, tools and site conditions vary widely. Although the editors have made every effort to ensure accuracy, the reader remains responsible for the selection and use of tools, materials and methods. Always obey local codes and laws, follow manufacturer instructions and observe safety precautions.

CONTENTS

1 OUTDOOR STORAGE

Storage bench

FOAM WEATHERSTRIP

A lift-up lid gives you tons of storage inside the bench. Foam weatherstrip keeps the interior fairly dry.

WHAT IT TAKES

TIME: 1 day
SKILL LEVEL: Beginner

Stash your stuff in this easy-to-build project

You can never have enough storage space, especially on a deck or patio, where there are no closets or cabinets. Although this bench won't be the answer to all your outdoor storage needs, it sure will help!

It's a place to tuck a bag of charcoal, stick a pair of work shoes, hide an extension cord or watering can and hey, you can even sit and take a breather on it, too.

Even if you've never taken on a woodworking project, you can build this bench. There is no fancy joinery holding it together, and you don't need special tools. The sides are 1x4s with sheet metal sandwiched between. The 1x4s intersect at the legs to create a strong joint. Drop in a plywood bottom and a hinged top, and you've got a sturdy attractive storage bench. It only takes about a day to build.

The tools are basic

You'll need a power miter saw (a circular saw with a speed square works, too), a jigsaw and a cordless drill. Clamps

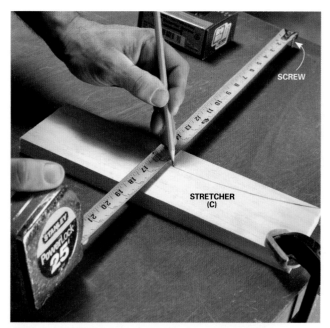

1 Draw an arc on each side stretcher by hooking a tape measure on a screw driven into the work surface. Draw the arcs on the legs using a compass or coffee can, then cut out all the arcs with your jigsaw.

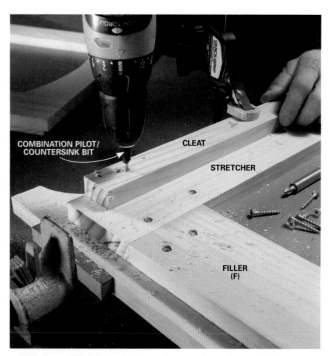

2 Clamp together the legs and outside stretchers to make a frame. Lay the sheet metal on it, then position the inside stretchers. Use a spacer to get the stretchers centered, then screw them on to lock everything together.

3 Screw filler pieces between the stretchers, then add cleats to hold the bottom. Be sure to predrill and countersink all screws.

aren't necessary, but they're very helpful. They'll hold the joints tight while you screw them together, and they provide an extra hand when you need it. If you don't have clamps, now might be the time to invest in a pair. The holes for the screws need to be predrilled and countersunk. A combination bit works best (Photo 3). Also have a nail set on hand (Photo 4).

Materials

This project is made primarily of 1x4s, and you can use just about any type of wood. Cedar, cypress or pine are great choices, but you'll need them smooth on all four sides. We used clear pine because it's straight and easy to work with, but it will need an annual coat of exterior stain, wood preservative or paint to protect it from the elements.

Sheet metal is used for the panels. Purchase it from a sheet metal shop or home center. You will need metal shears to cut it to size. We selected 24-gauge pre-finished steel ("Uniclad"), which is commonly used for flashing on buildings and is available in an array of colors. We used a copper color. If you prefer, cut the panels with tin snips from copper or galvanized roll flashing (available at home centers). Plywood forms the bottom and top of the bench. And 2- by 4-ft. sheets fit in a car better than full-size sheets.

Your first step: assemble the panels

Assemble all four sides in the same manner. Here's how:

Cut the legs and outside front stretchers to size from the Cutting List. Good square ends are essential, so if you're using a circular saw, use a speed square as a guide.

Lay out arcs (Photo 1) on the legs and outside stretchers (C), then cut out the curved pieces with a jigsaw. If you don't have a jigsaw or want a simpler look, cut a 60-degree angle on the legs and eliminate the arc on the stretchers.

Clamp the stretchers between the legs. Use a scrap piece of wood between the clamps and the legs to avoid denting your wood. Lay the sheet metal on the clamped boards, flush with the bottom and centered.

Figure A
Storage bench

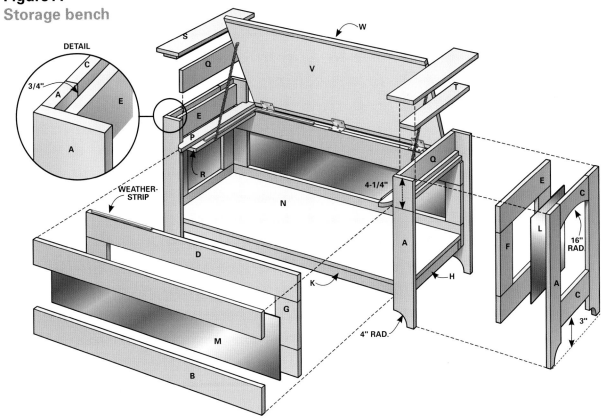

DETAIL

3/4"

WEATHER-STRIP

W

S

Q

V

T

E

P

R

N

4-1/4"

A

H

K

G

M

B

4" RAD.

E

L

F

A

C

C

16" RAD

3"

Cutting list

Overall Dimensions: 22-3/4"H x 50"W x 23"D

KEY	NAME	QTY.	DIMENSIONS	NOTES
A	Legs	8	1x4 x 22"	Cut arcs in feet
B	Outside front & back stretchers	4	1x4 x 41"	
C	Outside side stretchers	4	1x4 x 12-1/2"	Cut arcs in two of them
D	Inside front stretchers	4	1x4 x 46-1/2"	Measure from bench
E	Inside side stretchers	4	1x4 x 18"	Measure from bench
F	Inside side fillers	4	1x4 x 11-1/4"	Measure from bench
G	Inside front & back fillers	4	1x4 x 7-3/4"	Measure from bench
H	Side cleats	2	1x2 x 16-1/4"	Measure from bench
K	Front & back cleats	2	1x2 x 44-3/4"	Measure from bench
L	Side panels	2	17-3/4" x 18"	24 gauge sheet metal
M	Front & back panels	2	46" x 14-1/2"	24 gauge sheet metal
N	Bottom (1/2" plywood)	1	45" x 18"	Measure from bench
P	Arm supports	2	1x4 x 21-1/2"	Cut notches and round corners
Q	Arm fillers	2	1x4 x 19-1/2"	
R	Lid supports	2	1x4 x 18"	Measure from bench
S	Arms	2	1x6 x 23"	
T	Cleats	2	1 x 19-1/2" x 2"	Rip to fit, measure from bench
V	Lid (3/4" plywood)	1	20-1/4" x 37-3/4"	Measure from bench
W	Molding	2	3/4" x 3/4" x 37-3/4"	Measure from bench

Materials list

1	roll of galvanized steel flashing (12' x 18" wide)

Wood

10	1x4 - 8'
1	1x6 - 6'
2	1x2 - 8'
1	2'x4' 1/2" BC plywood
1	2'x4' 3/4" BC plywood
1	3/4" x 3/4" square molding

Hardware

1 lb	1-1/4"x #8 exterior screws
1 lb	2" galvanized casing nails
3	3" butt hinges
4	small eye screws
4'	lightweight chain
12'	1/2" weatherstrip
	Exterior glue

4 Nail the front, back and sides together. Predrill for each nail, and drive the nail heads slightly below the surface with a nail set. For additional strength, run a bead of glue along each joint before assembling.

NAIL SET

5 Mark the notches for the arm supports directly from the bench. Cut out the notches with a jigsaw, then round off the protruding corners.

FLUSH HERE

ARM SUPPORT (P)

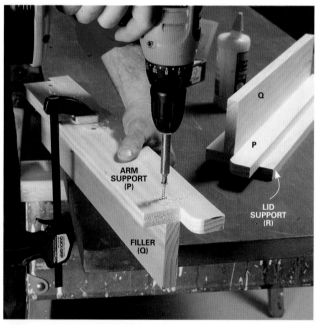

6 Clamp the arm support to the filler piece, screw them together, then add the lid support.

ARM SUPPORT (P)

LID SUPPORT (R)

FILLER (Q)

Q

P

Cut one inside stretcher, then lay it on top of the clamped-together frame, as shown in Photo 2. Center it on the frame; it will be narrower than the width of the frame. It's important that the gap at each end equals the thickness of your wood plus the sheet metal. Adjust the length if necessary and cut the remaining inside stretchers. Screw them all in place, remembering to keep the inside stretchers on the sides 3/4 in. from the top edge (see Figure A, detail). The lower stretcher is flush to the bottom. Use 1-1/4-in. deck screws, predrilled and countersunk. Position the screws so they're sure to catch the front 1x4s; because of the offset, it's easy to miss.

Add filler pieces (F) between stretchers, then add the 1x2 cleats (H and K) that'll hold the bench bottom (Photo 3). Repeat this process for the other three panels.

Nail the panels together

The toughest part of nailing the panels together is holding them in place. Here's where a clamp really helps. Clamp a side panel inside the front and back panels, flush up all the edges and gently tighten the clamp. This is a bit of a juggling act, so you may want to call for someone to help. Place a piece of wood or cardboard between the jaws and the legs to avoid denting the wood (Photo 4). Predrill 3/32-in. holes, then glue and nail the corners with 2-in. galvanized finish nails. Reposition the clamp as you nail to keep the joints tight. Repeat at the other end.

Measure the bottom and cut a piece of plywood to fit. When you drop in the bottom, it will square up the bench. Predrill, countersink, glue and screw the bottom to the cleats.

The arm assembly

This assembly looks a little complicated, but it's really not. It's made up of three pieces, which are measured from the bench (Photo 5) and cut to fit. After you notch the arm supports, round off the front ends shown in Photo 7 (so they won't catch a pant leg), then temporarily set them in place. Hold the lid supports (R) in place underneath the arm supports and mark. Fit and nail the two assemblies to the bench.

Fastening a cleat to the bottom of each arm (Photo 8) lets

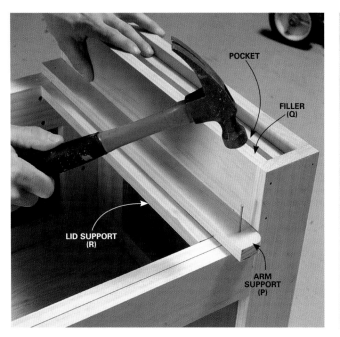

7 Place the arm assembly in position and nail it to the legs and stretcher. There will be a pocket formed at the top where the arm cleat will go (see next photo).

8 Attach a cleat to the underside of each arm, using diagonal lines to center it. Place the arms on the bench and nail through the cleats to secure them.

you hide nails on the sides of the bench when you attach them. Measure the width of the opening of the arm and rip (cut the long way) the cleat (T) to fit. Although not the quickest, your jigsaw is the safest tool for this cut. Attach the cleats to the arms (Photo 8), then nail the arms to the bench.

The lid

Installing the lid can be a bit awkward. Here are a few techniques that'll make it go easier:

Cut the plywood 1/4 in. shorter than the width of the opening, so the lid closes easily. Then glue and nail two pieces of molding (W) to cover the exposed edges of the plywood. Place the lid on the workbench and attach the hinges to the lid. We used no-mortise hinges, but any butt hinge will work.

Flip the bench on its back with its arms overhanging each side of your workbench (Photo 9). Put a couple of 1-in. blocks under it to raise it to the level of the lid, center it, then screw on the hinge.

A few remaining details

Install a pair of screw eyes and attach a chain to keep the lid from falling back. Then place a band of foam weatherstrip around the perimeter to help keep out the rain. Finally, bore a dozen 3/8-in. ventilation holes in the bottom.

Seal the bench with a coat of deck stain and preservative. If it's used outdoors, the bench will need a fresh coat annually. And if you're like most folks, you'll have to clean it out once a year, too, because it's sure to fill up fast.

9 Fasten the hinges to the bench. Rest the bench on its back, on top of 1-inch blocks, center the lid in the opening, then screw it on. Give the whole bench a once-over with sandpaper, and you're ready to finish!

Remote garden storage

WHAT IT TAKES

TIME: 3 hours
SKILL LEVEL: Beginner

Figure A
Exploded view

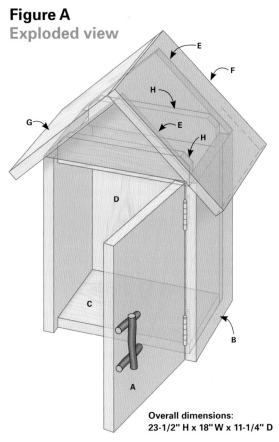

Overall dimensions:
23-1/2" H x 18" W x 11-1/4" D

Keep tools and supplies right next to your garden with this small storage house. It only takes a few hours to build, and can be made with pine or rough-sawn cedar as shown here.

Cut flat, dry 1x12s to the sizes in the Cutting List. Nail and glue the sides, base and back together, then attach the rafters and gables.

Fasten the shorter roof panel on one side, leaving 7/8-in. overhangs in the front and back. Caulk the top edge, then nail the long panel on.

Cut the hinge mortises into the door and side, and hang the door. Stain or paint the wood inside and out to seal it. Use green branches for the handle, nailing them in place.

Make a rustic door handle from a tree branch. Nail the crosspieces to the door with brad nails, then notch the back of the handle so it sits flat on the crosspieces and nail it in place.

Cutting list

KEY	QTY.	SIZE & DESCRIPTION
A	1	11" x 15-3/4" door
B	2	9-1/2" x 15-7/8" sides
C	1	11-1/4" x 8" bottom
D	1	11-1/4" x 15-7/8" back
E	2	12-3/4" x 6-1/2" gables
F	1	11-1/4" x 12-3/4" long roof panel
G	1	11-1/4" x 12" short roof panel
H	2	11-1/4" x 2-1/2" rafters

Note: All dimensions are for 3/4"-thick wood.

Materials list

QTY.	ITEM
2	1x12 x 8' cedar or pine
1	4x4 x 8' post
1 pr.	2" x 2" mortise hinges
1	Magnetic catch
1 lb.	1-1/2" galvanized finish nails

Garden tool cabinet

WHAT IT TAKES

TIME: 1 weekend
SKILL LEVEL: Intermediate

Give your garden tools their own home so they're easy to find

I magine this: You drive home with a carload of new plants and flowers. You open your new outdoor garden tool cabinet and grab your shovel, bulb planter, trimmer or whatever you need—and it's all there in plain view! This scenario doesn't have to be a dream. You can build this cabinet in one weekend and paint and organize it the next.

This cabinet is compact, but it can store all of your garden hand tools and still have room for boots, fertilizers and accessories. Most gardeners set aside a tiny spot in their garage for their tools, which often end up tangled in a corner. Now your garden tools can have a home of their own, outside the garage. The design is flexible, so you can customize the interior to suit your needs and add a lock if you wish.

Here you'll learn how to assemble the cabinet in your garage and then wheel it out and mount it on your garage wall. And you don't have to be a crackerjack carpenter or own special tools to build it.

Besides being good looking, this project is designed to last. The shingled roof will keep the rain out. And if moisture does get in, the slatted bottom and

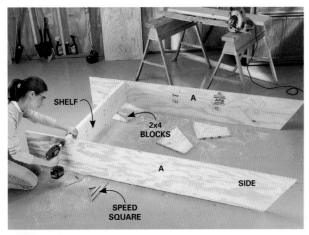

1 Cut the plywood sides and 2x10 shelf, prop up the shelf with 2x4 blocks and fasten the sides into the shelf with 2-in. deck screws.

2 Turn the assembly over and screw the back to the sides and center shelf. Use a level or straightedge to mark the shelf location on the back side of the plywood.

3 Cut the subrails (D) and the roof supports (H), then screw them into place. Use 2-in. screws for the subrails and 3-in. screws for the roof supports.

4 Glue and nail the 1x2 cleats (E and F) to the sides, back and subrail (D) and then screw the 1x4 floor slats (G) to the cleats. Start with the center slat and leave 7/16-in. gaps.

4-in.-diameter vents near the top allow enough air circulation to dry everything out. This storage cabinet was mounted on the outside of a garage, but you can easily mount it to the back of your house or to a shed.

The 4-ft. by nearly 8-ft. cabinet is made from exterior plywood with pine trim. All the materials are available at home centers and lumberyards. You can find a huge variety of tool mounting clips and retainers at hardware stores for hanging rakes, shovels, clippers and everything else. Just let your imagination solve the need. So what are you waiting for? Get the materials, read the photo sequence, examine the detailed drawings and text instructions, and get started.

Assemble the main box

Exterior-grade plywood is the basic building material for this project. Unfortunately, you'll never find *absolutely* flat pieces of plywood at a home center or lumberyard, but the flatter you can find them, the better this project will turn out. Choose a BC grade

5 Mount the 1x2 roof trim to the 3/4-in. plywood roof, then center it and mark the position. Then temporarily screw it to the roof supports with a pair of 2-in. screws on each side.

Figure A Garden tool cabinet

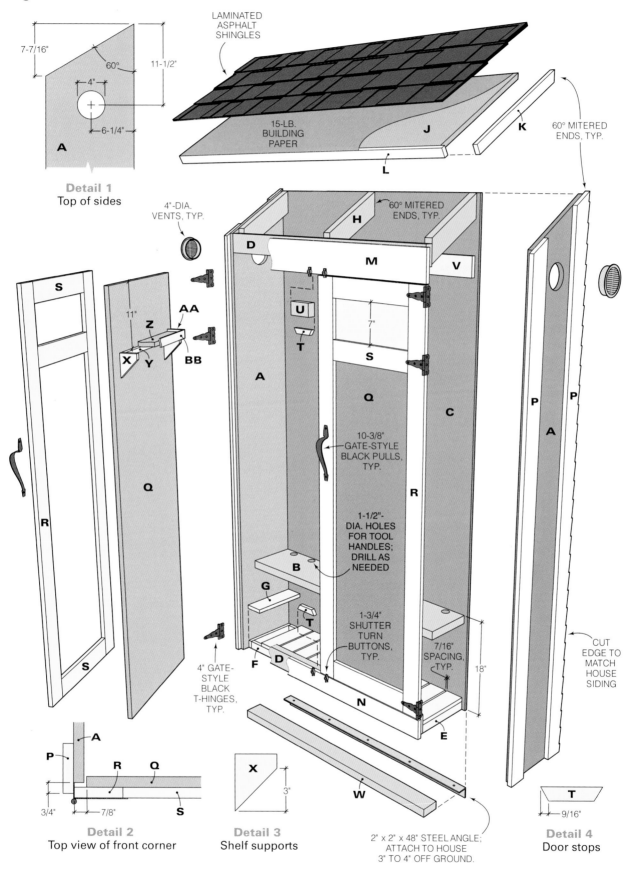

Detail 1
Top of sides

7-7/16"
60°
11-1/2"
4"
6-1/4"
A

LAMINATED
ASPHALT
SHINGLES

15-LB.
BUILDING
PAPER

J

K

L

60° MITERED
ENDS, TYP.

4"-DIA.
VENTS, TYP.

60° MITERED
ENDS, TYP.

D   H

M   V

U
T

S

A

11"
Z   AA
X Y   BB

Q

A

7"

S

Q

C

R

10-3/8"
GATE-STYLE
BLACK PULLS,
TYP.

1-1/2"-
DIA. HOLES
FOR TOOL
HANDLES;
DRILL AS
NEEDED

B

G

T

R

S

F D

4" GATE-
STYLE
BLACK
T-HINGES,
TYP.

1-3/4"
SHUTTER
TURN
BUTTONS,
TYP.

7/16"
SPACING,
TYP.

18"

N

E

CUT
EDGE TO
MATCH
HOUSE
SIDING

P   P

A

W

2" x 2" x 48" STEEL ANGLE;
ATTACH TO HOUSE
3" TO 4" OFF GROUND.

Detail 2
Top view of front corner

A
P
R   Q
3/4"   7/8"   S

Detail 3
Shelf supports

X
3"

Detail 4
Door stops

T
9/16"

of plywood. This will ensure you have one good side "B" that'll look good on the outside, and the "C" side can go inside.

Once you get the plywood home, keep it out of the sun or your flat panel will turn into a tortilla chip in no time. It's best to cut the pieces in the shade or in your garage. A long straightedge cutting guide for your circular saw will help you get nice straight cuts if you don't have a full-size table saw. Look at the Cutting List below and cut all the parts to size except the door stiles, rails and trim pieces, which are best cut to fit once you've constructed the main plywood box.

Choose the flattest sheet of 3/4-in. plywood for the door cores. As you lay out all the pieces, choose the best-looking side of the plywood for the painted parts. The sides of the cabinet form a 30-degree slope for the roof. Use a Speed square (see Photo 1) to mark the angled roof supports (H) and ends of the trim pieces that follow the roofline. It's easier to cut accurate slopes on the larger side pieces (A) by first measuring each side, marking a diagonal line from point to point and then cutting along the mark. Assemble the main box of the cabinet as shown in Figure A and Photos 1 – 5. Drill pilot holes for all screws with a No. 8 combination countersink and pilot bit. Use 2-in. galvanized deck screws to fasten the sides to the shelf and 1-5/8-in. screws to fasten the back to the sides.

Cut the roof panel (J) and trim pieces (K and L), then glue and nail the trim to the front and side edges of the roof panel. Center the panel (Photo 5) and temporarily screw it to the roof supports so you can install the side trim (P) and the upper rail (M). Note: You'll need to remove the roof and the doors after assembly to make the project light enough to move to your site.

Keeping critters out

Cut a piece of 1/4-in. hardware cloth to fit under the floor slats of the cabinet. This wire mesh will keep furry critters from making your tool cabinet into a cozy winter home.

6 Glue and screw the 1x4 side trim to the plywood sides, keeping the trim pieces 3/4 in. proud at the front. Cut the 4-in.-diameter side vents.

Materials list

ITEM	QTY.
3/4" x 4' x 8' BC plywood	2
1/2" x 4' x 8' BC plywood	1
2x10 x 4' pine	1
2x4 x 8' pine	2
1x6 x 8' pine	1
1x4 x 8' pine	12
1x2 x 8' pine	3
2x4 x 8' treated wood	1
12" x 48" hardware cloth (1/4" grid)	1
Bundle of asphalt shingles	1
3' x 5' strip of 15-lb. building paper	1
1-5/8" galv. screws	2 lbs.
2" galv. screws	2 lbs.
3" galv. screws	1 lbs.
4" T-hinges	6
Shutter turn buttons	4
4" round vents	2
1-1/4" finish nails	1 lb.
1/4" x 3" galv. lag screws and washers	9
2" x 2" steel angle	1
7/8" shingle nails	1 lb.

Cutting list

KEY	QTY.	SIZE & DESCRIPTION
A	2	3/4" x 12-7/8" x 90" plywood sides
B	1	1-1/2" x 9-1/4" x 46-1/2" pine shelf
C	1	1/2" x 48" x 90" plywood back
D	2	1-1/2" x 3-1/2" x 46-1/2" pine subrails
E	2	3/4" x 1-1/2" x 11-3/8" pine bottom cleats
F	2	3/4" x 1-1/2" x 45" pine bottom cleats
G	12	3/4" x 3-1/2" x 11-3/8" pine bottom slat
H	3	1-1/2" x 3-1/2" x 15-1/8" pine roof supports
J	1	3/4" x 21-7/8" x 60" plywood roof
K	2	3/4" x 1-1/2" x 21-7/8" pine roof trim
L	1	3/4" x 1-1/2" x 61-1/2" pine roof trim
M	1	3/4" x 5-1/2" x 48" pine upper rail
N	1	3/4" x 3-1/2" x 48" pine lower rail
P	4	3/4" x 3-1/2" x 91" pine side trim
Q	2	3/4" x 23" x 72-3/4" plywood doors
R	4	3/4" x 3-1/2" x 72-3/4" pine door stile
S	6	3/4" x 3-1/2" x 16-7/8" pine door rail trim
T	2	3/4" x 1" x 4-1/2" pine door stop
U	1	1-1/2" x 2-7/16" x 4-1/2" pine door stop support
V	1	3/4" x 3-1/2" x 46-1/2"pine hang rail
W	1	1-1/2" x 3-1/2" x 48" treated mounting board
X	1	3/4" x 3" x 4" pine shelf supports
Y	1	3/4" x 3/4" x 16-1/2" pine shelf-mounting cleat
Z	1	3/4" x 3" x 20" pine shelf
AA	2	1/4" x 1-1/2" x 3" pine shelf edging
BB	1	1/4" x 1-1/2" x 20-1/2" pine shelf edging

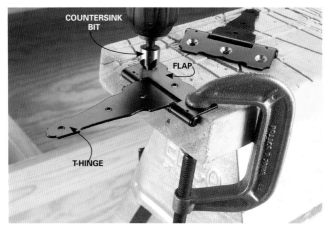

7 Countersink the holes in the inside of the hinge flaps to accept the tapered heads of the mounting screws.

8 Position the flaps of the hinges against the plywood sides at the centers of the door rail locations. Drill pilot holes and drive the screws into the side trim to secure the hinges.

Add trim and assemble the doors

Make sure to extend the front edge of each side. Set the trim (P) 3/4 in. beyond the front edge of the plywood side (Photo 6). Next cut and nail the front upper rail (M) and the lower rail (N) to the subrails. Both ends should butt tightly to the side trim.

Even though the doors are made mainly from plywood, the rail and stile trim boards glued and screwed to the front side give the doors a handsome frame-and-panel look. Be sure to lay the doors out on a flat surface and then glue and nail the rails (short horizontal pieces) and stiles (long vertical pieces) to the plywood surface. The stile on each hinge side must hang 3/4 in. past the plywood (see Photo 10 inset).

You'll need to alter the factory T-hinge for the inset design of the doors. The hinge flap is screwed to the side trim (P) as shown in Photo 8. If you were to use the factory-supplied pan head screws, the door would bind on the screw heads. To solve this problem, taper the edges of the existing holes with a countersink bit. Remove just enough steel (Photo 7) so the head of the tapered No. 8 x 3/4-in. screw fits flush with the hinge flap surface.

Cut the small doorstops with a handsaw and then glue and nail them to the edges of the subrails. With the doorstops in place, set the doors into the opening. Make sure you leave a 1/8-in. gap at the top and bottom and a 3/16-in. gap between the doors. You may need to plane or belt-sand the door edges to get a good fit. Note: Because the flaps of the hinge that fasten to the side trim are about 7/8 in. wide instead of 3/4 in., your doors will sit about 1/8 in. proud of the side trim.

Mount the cabinet to the wall

Fasten a 4-ft. 2x4 to the top flange of a 4-ft.-long piece of steel angle (Figure A). At a hardware store, you can usually find steel angle that measures 1-1/2 in. x 1-1/2 in. with holes drilled every 3 in., but any steel angle that's 1/8 in. thick or larger will do.

Locate the exact position of your cabinet on the wall at least 3 in. above grade and then fasten the angle to the wall with 1/4-in. galvanized lag screws. It must be level. You may need to cut a course or two of siding to get the angle to lie flat. This garage slab was several inches off the ground, so holes were drilled into the side of the slab, lag shields were installed and the angle was fastened. If your slab is too close to the ground, you can fasten the angle farther up into the wood studs of the garage. The weight of your cabinet rests entirely on this steel angle. It's not necessary to fasten the bottom of the cabinet to it.

Measure the locations of the wall studs and transfer these to the cabinet back. Locate three 1/4-in.-diameter pilot holes in the hang rail (V) and another three holes 4 in. up from the bottom at the stud locations.

Now, strap your cabinet to a furniture dolly (with the doors and roof removed to reduce the weight) and wheel it over to the steel angle. Set the bottom of the cabinet onto the steel angle, center it and temporarily brace it against the wall. Drill 5/32-in.-diameter pilot holes into the wall studs using the existing pilot holes as a guide. Drive the 3-in. lag screws (including washers) and snug the cabinet to the wall.

Finishing touches

Lay the side trim (P) against the siding. You may need to trim it with your jigsaw to conform (Photo 12). Screw the roof panel to the cabinet. Staple a layer of 15-lb. building paper to the roof panel and shingle the panel using 7/8-in. roofing nails. Avoid driving shingle nails through the overhangs where the points might show. When you get to the last course, trim the shingles to fit and run a bead of matching caulk at the siding to seal the edge.

Rehang the doors and then mount the door handles and the catches at the top and bottom of the door. Wait to add your vents until you've finished painting. The vents shown here were spray-painted to match the color of the sides.

Take a trip to the hardware store and shop for a variety of fasteners, from angle screws to rake and broom holders. Once you finish organizing the cabinet, prime it and then paint it to match your siding.

7/8" OVERHANG ON SIDE

S R Q R S Q R

9 Glue and nail the door rail and stile trim to the 3/4-in. plywood core. Overhang the stile on the hinge side of each door 7/8 in. See Figure A for the exact placement.

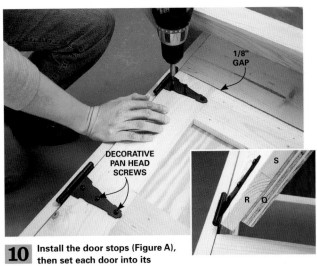

1/8" GAP

DECORATIVE PAN HEAD SCREWS

S R Q

10 Install the door stops (Figure A), then set each door into its opening. Use the decorative pan head screws provided by the manufacturer for the long decorative flap on the door surface.

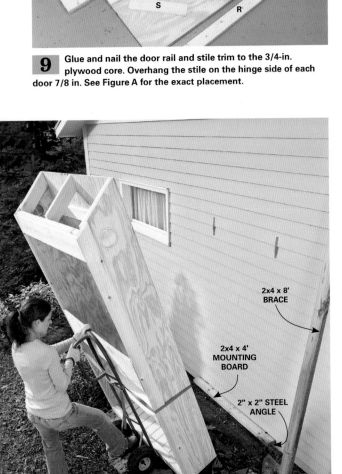

2x4 x 8' BRACE

2x4 x 4' MOUNTING BOARD

2" x 2" STEEL ANGLE

11 Fasten a steel angle to the foundation with a 2x4 attached to its top (Figure A). Lift the cabinet into place and stabilize it with a 8-ft. 2x4 brace against the ground, forcing the cabinet back against the wall.

P P

NOTCHES FOR SIDING

2x4 BRACE

12 Scribe the 1x4 side trim to fit the siding. Cut the notches with a jigsaw. Nail it to the cabinet side. Screw on the roof panel and shingle it.

Alternate siding materials

If you have vinyl, aluminum or steel siding, here's how to prevent the siding from deforming as you tighten the cabinet to the wall. Instead of tightening the lag screws one at a time, gently tighten them alternately to even out the pressure as you go.

Rustic garden toolbox

Figure A

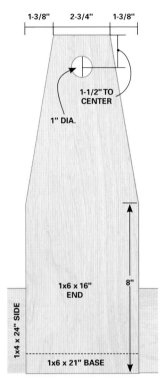

1-3/8" 2-3/4" 1-3/8"

1-1/2" TO CENTER

1" DIA.

1x6 x 16" END

1x4 x 24" SIDE

8"

1x6 x 21" BASE

This simple gardening toolbox gets its natural charm from the branches used for the sides and handle. When you're searching for branches, choose green, freshly cut ones for strength and flexibility. The only tools required are a saw and a drill and maybe a knife to whittle the handle ends.

Along with three 25-in.-long branches, you'll need a 6-ft. 1x6, a 4-ft. 1x4 and a short length of 1/4-in. wood dowel, exterior wood glue and a handful of 1-5/8-in. deck screws. We used clear pine, but No. 2 pine or cedar will work fine too.

Cut the parts using Figure A as a guide. Then screw the box together (Photo 1). Whittle the handle ends to fit the holes. You'll have to bend the handle to slip it into the second hole.

Cut away any knobs on the branches for the sides. Then attach them, keeping the screws at least an inch from the ends to avoid splits (Photo 2). Finally, drill 1/4-in. holes through the handle ends and drive in the dowels to hold the handle in place (Photo 3).

1-1/2" INSET

1-5/8" DECK SCREW

1 Screw the box together with deck screws. Predrill and countersink the screws to avoid splitting.

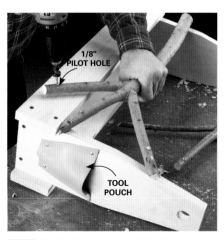

1/8" PILOT HOLE

TOOL POUCH

2 Cut the branch ends to fit. Attach the pieces to the sides of the toolbox with screws or nails. Predrill to avoid splitting.

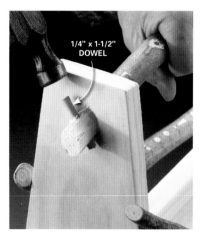

1/4" x 1-1/2" DOWEL

3 Drill 1/4-in. holes through the handle ends and drive in the dowels to hold the handle in place.

2 GARDEN PLANTERS

Privacy trellis with planters

WHAT IT TAKES

TIME: 1 day
SKILL LEVEL: Beginner

For privacy and more greenery, build a trellis with removeable planter boxes. You can adapt this design to fencing (or a section of fencing), the side of a deck, an arbor or pergola. Or you can make a stand-alone trellis in your yard.

The trellis shown here is adapted to an existing pergola, and is built from 1x4s and a center 2x4. The boards are screwed to the 2x4 and the sides with 1 5/8-in. deck screws. The planter boxes are sized to hold four 6-in. plastic pots. Build as many as you want and just hang them from the 1x4s.

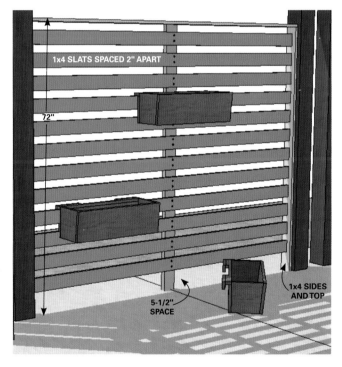

Figure A
Privacy trellis

1x4 SLATS SPACED 2" APART

72"

5-1/2" SPACE

1x4 SIDES AND TOP

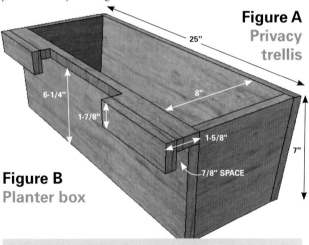

Figure B
Planter box

25"

6-1/4"

8"

1-7/8"

1-5/8"

7/8" SPACE

7"

Cutting list: Privacy trellis

KEY	QTY.	SIZE & DESCRIPTION
A	2	3/4" x 3-1/2" x 71-1/4" (vertical sides)
B	1	3/4" x 3-1/2" x 92" (horizontal top)
C	1	1-1/2" x 3-1/2" x 71-1/4" (center support)
D	12	3/4" x 3-1/2" x 90-1/2" (horizontal slats)

Materials list: Privacy trellis and planter box

ITEM	QTY.
1x4 x 8' treated pine	15
2x4 x 8' treated pine	1
1x8 x 10' cedar (per planter box)	1
No. 8 x 1-5/8" self-drilling exterior screws	50
1-3/4" galvanized nails (for planter box assembly)	1 box
Exterior construction adhesive (for planter assembly)	1 tube

Bamboo planter & trellis

Bring flowers and foliage to your deck or patio

If you're wishing for wisteria or craving clematis, you can plant them just steps away in this planter and trellis for your deck or patio. And if you build a pair of them, you can create a privacy screen or provide shade from the late afternoon sun.

In one weekend you can build this planter/trellis combination for less than half the cost of a similar one—made of wood or plastic—at a garden center.

To build this planter, you'll need standard woodworking tools like a table saw and a miter saw. If you want to round the edges of the wooden parts as we did, you'll also need a router and two round-over bits (1/4- and 1/2-in. radius). Your cost for materials will depend mostly on the wood you choose for the planter box. We built our planter from "select-grade" pine boards. If you don't mind a few knots, use construction-grade pine, which costs less. If you live in a damp climate, consider rot-resistant choices like cedar or teak. Pressure-treated lumber is another good choice because it costs about the same as construction-grade pine and lasts practically forever. The drawback is that you may have to let it dry for a month before you start building.

Small-diameter bamboo for the planter box slats and lattice is in stock at most home centers and garden centers. The bamboo we used was labeled "3/4 inch." To find 1-1/2-in.-diameter bamboo for the trellis posts and header, visit a large garden center or shop online (search for "bamboo poles"). Select straight poles for the trellis posts and header. You'll find lower prices online, but those savings may be offset by shipping charges.

Master a new material

Bamboo is one of the world's greatest building materials. It's incredibly strong, good-looking and cheap. And if you're a weekend woodworker, you already have the tools to work with it. But bamboo doesn't behave exactly like wood, so you'll also need some new tricks up your sleeve. We'll show you how to build with this hard and brittle, irregular and hollow material.

1 **Build four frames.** Glue together the frames that form the sides of the planter box. Clamp a framing square to your workbench to help align the parts.

BACK OF FRAME

2 **Mask the frames.** Line the backs of the frames with wide masking tape. When you finish the wood later, the tape will keep stain off the bamboo.

3 **Glue on the bamboo.** Fill the frames with bamboo slats. Screw the first slat in place and set the rest in heavy beads of construction adhesive.

4 **Assemble the planter box.** First screw the frames together at the corners. Then screw on the legs from inside the box and add the floor and top rim.

5 **Build the lattice on a frame.** Screw the first layer of bamboo poles directly to the frame, using spacer blocks to position them. Drill a pilot hole for every screw; bamboo splits easily.

6 **Wire the lattice together.** Tie the second layer of bamboo to the first with wire ties. Twist until the looped ends snap off. Then bend the remaining wire flat against the bamboo.

Build the planter box

To get started, rip four 8-ft.-long 1x6s into strips on your table saw. You'll need two 2-3/4-in.-wide strips for the top rim, two 1-3/4-in.-wide strips for the cleats and legs, and four 2-1/2-in.-wide strips for the legs, rails and stiles. Glue the rails and stiles together to make frames (Photo 1). Sand the frames and round the inside edges with your router and a 1/4-in. round-over bit. Then mask around the frames (Photo 2).

You'll need to cut about 120 slats to fill the frames. To avoid measuring them all, clamp a stop block next to your miter saw. With the slats cut, mark guidelines 1-1/4 in. from the top and bottom of the frames and glue the slats between them (Photo 3). Place the best side of each slat face down. Alternate thin and thick slats, and the direction of the tapers—one narrow end up, the next down.

While you're waiting for the adhesive to harden, glue together the planter legs. Round the edges with a 1/2-in. round-over bit.

Assemble the planter box (Photo 4). Take diagonal corner-to-corner measurements to make sure the box is square before you screw the pressure-treated

Figure A
Bamboo planter & trellis

Overall dimensions:
40 in. wide x 18 in. deep
x 72 in. tall. All wood
parts are 3/4 in. thick.

Bamboo parts vary
in diameter from
3/8 to 3/4 in. unless
otherwise noted.

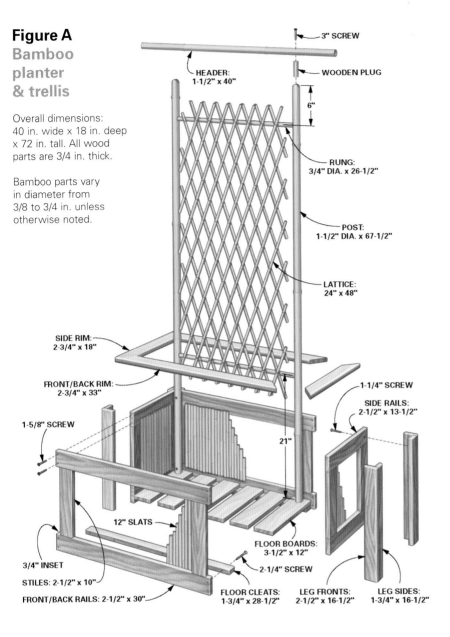

- 3" SCREW
- HEADER: 1-1/2" x 40"
- WOODEN PLUG
- 6"
- RUNG: 3/4" DIA. x 26-1/2"
- POST: 1-1/2" DIA. x 67-1/2"
- LATTICE: 24" x 48"
- SIDE RIM: 2-3/4" x 18"
- FRONT/BACK RIM: 2-3/4" x 33"
- 1-5/8" SCREW
- 1-1/4" SCREW
- SIDE RAILS: 2-1/2" x 13-1/2"
- 21"
- 12" SLATS
- FLOOR BOARDS: 3-1/2" x 12"
- 3/4" INSET
- 2-1/4" SCREW
- STILES: 2-1/2" x 10"
- FRONT/BACK RAILS: 2-1/2" x 30"
- FLOOR CLEATS: 1-3/4" x 28-1/2"
- LEG FRONTS: 2-1/2" x 16-1/2"
- LEG SIDES: 1-3/4" x 16-1/2"

floor boards to the cleats. Top off the planter box with rim boards, mitered at the corners and screwed to the frames. We rounded the edges of our rim material with a 1/4-in. round-over bit before cutting it to length. The rim over hangs the inside of the box by 1/2 in.

Build the trellis

To assemble the lattice, first grab any 1x4s or 2x4s you have handy and build a 1x4 frame with inner dimensions of 2 x 4 ft. Take diagonal corner-to-corner measurements to make sure the frame is square. Lay the first pole across the frame from one corner to the other and screw it to the frame. Then add more poles, screwing each to the frame (Photo 5). Although it's time-consuming, you must drill a pilot hole for every screw—otherwise, the bamboo will split.

Attach the second layer of bamboo with wire ties and a "twister" tool (Photo 6). Wire ties are designed to connect the rebar that reinforces concrete, so you'll find them and a twister in the masonry aisle at home centers. For a neat, tight connection, pull upward on the twister as it spins. When the lattice is done, cut it out of the frame (Photo 7).

Next, build the bamboo frame that will hold the lattice. Start by cutting kerfs in the posts and header (Photo 8). Bamboo can develop wide cracks as it dries out. Cutting a kerf creates a single, straight opening and prevents random splitting. Then cut the tops of the posts

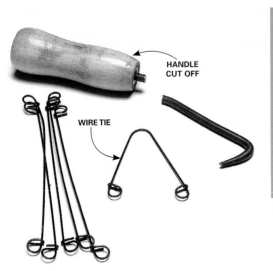

HANDLE CUT OFF

WIRE TIE

Using wire ties

Wire ties are simple to use: Bend each tie in half and slip it over the bamboo. Then hook the looped ends with the twister tool and spin. For faster twisting, cut the handle off the tool and chuck it into a drill (Photo 6).

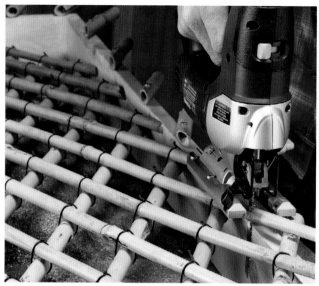

7 Cut out the lattice. Trim the completed lattice off the frame by guiding a jigsaw or reciprocating saw along the inner edge of the frame.

SAW KERF

8 Prevent cracks with kerfs. Cut saw kerfs in the posts and header. This prevents random cracks from developing later. To cut safely, screw the bamboo to a 2x4.

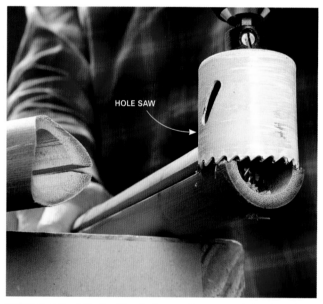

HOLE SAW

9 Cut "saddles" with a hole saw. Create rounded ends on the trellis posts to hold the header. For a clean cut, run the drill at high speed and apply light pressure.

POST

RUNG

PLUG INSIDE

HEADER

10 Screw on the header. Screw the header to the posts. Drill pilot holes to avoid splitting the bamboo. Attach the lattice to the rungs using wire ties.

using a 1-1/2-in. hole saw (Photo 9). Glue 4-in.-long 3/4 x 3/4-in. wooden plugs into the posts to provide anchors for the screws that fasten the header. The plugs don't have to fit tight; just use lots of construction adhesive.

Drill the posts with a 3/4-in. hole saw to create sockets for the rungs. Don't use a spade bit; the bamboo will split. Insert the rungs and measure the spread of the posts. To fit into the planter box, the spread must be no more than 27-1/2

in. Cut the rungs a bit shorter if needed and then glue them into the posts with construction adhesive. Attach the header (Photo 10). Leave the trellis frame on a flat surface until the adhesive hardens, then attach the lattice to the rungs. When you screw the completed trellis to the planter box, insert wooden blocks behind the bottom ends of the posts. Bamboo isn't perfectly straight, so you'll have to experiment with blocks of different thicknesses to make the posts plumb.

We finished our planter box with deck stain. When you're done finishing, slice the masking tape around the box frames with a utility knife and peel off the tape. Add plastic furniture glides to the legs to keep the wood from soaking up moisture. To hold soil, we used a 12-1/2-in. x 27-in. plastic planter. You could use two or three smaller pots instead.

Make a bamboo teepee

Climbing plants add an attractive third dimension to gardens. And the good news is that they don't care if their support is a pricey architectural statement or a couple of sticks.

A "teepee" made of bamboo stakes fits right in with a country flower or vegetable garden. It's cheap and simple to build and store. All you need are twine and some 3/4-in.-dia. bamboo stakes. Plunge the stakes (three or more, depending on how big you want it) into the soil so they form a teepee when the tops are bound together with twine as shown. Annual vines from beans and peas to morning glories will scramble up just about any support and quickly cover it up (inset photo), so if this bamboo doesn't look attractive to begin with, just wait a few weeks.

WHAT IT TAKES

TIME: 30 minutes
SKILL LEVEL: Beginner

Hardy street-side planter

Life on the street is tough on plants, too. They must survive exhaust fumes, heat and light reflected from the pavement, cramped roots, and winter road salt. In these areas, start with street-tough plants such as salvia, ornamental oregano, cranesbill geranium and sedum. But even these plants benefit from some extra attention.

Enriching the soil quality is essential. Do this by elevating the bed with timbers and adding a 3-in.-thick layer of mulch to conserve soil moisture and protect roots. Water these plants frequently and deeply. Also, hose off the foliage to remove dust, soot and salt, being sure to spray even the underside of the leaves.

WHAT IT TAKES

TIME: 4 hours
SKILL LEVEL: Beginner

3" LAYER OF SHREDDED WOOD MULCH

4x4 LANDSCAPE TIMBER

6x6 LANDSCAPE TIMBER

Arched planter

Bend wood to create this graceful plant stand. You can make it with only two boards!

With this elegant curved deck planter, you can have a splash of garden anyplace you like. Deck it out with flower pots and accent your patio, deck or front steps.

Here, we'll show you how to build the whole project in a leisurely weekend. Bending wood strips into laminated arches may seem challenging, but we'll walk you through the process step by step. After you build your first planter, you'll have the hang of it, and the next one will be a cinch to build. The key, as you'll see, is a simple plywood "bending" jig that you can use over and over again.

You can complete this project if you're handy with basic carpentry tools. However, you'll need a table saw equipped with a thin-kerf blade for ripping the strips and other parts. Sorry, but a circular saw just won't do the job no matter how steady you are. But you'll still need a circular saw, as well as a belt sander and at least four 3-ft. pipe or bar clamps (Photo 4).

Select wood with small, tight knots

You only need two 8-ft.-long 2x8s for the entire project. Our planter is made from western red cedar, chosen for its beauty and natural decay resistance. But any wood you choose will be fine as long as you select straight boards with small, tight knots. The long thin strips will break at large knots during the bending process. You'll be using nearly every inch of each board, so pick ones without splits or cracks at the ends. It may take some sorting at the home center, but the effort's worth it.

While you're at the home center, pick up 2 qts. of exterior woodworking glue along with a mini paint roller (Photo 6), a 4 x 8-ft. sheet of 3/4-in. plywood and a 10-ft. x 20-ft. roll of "painter's" plastic (3 mil). Also buy a small box of galvanized 1-in. brads if you intend to hand-nail. Or, if you have an air nailer (Photo 11), get brads for your nail gun.

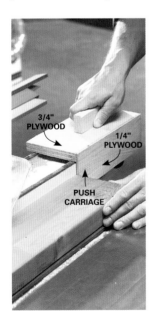

1 Cut the 2x8s to length following Figure A. Rip 5/16-in.-wide strips for the arches and the slats. Build a push carriage sized to fit your fence to safely cut thin strips.

3/4" PLYWOOD
1/4" PLYWOOD
PUSH CARRIAGE

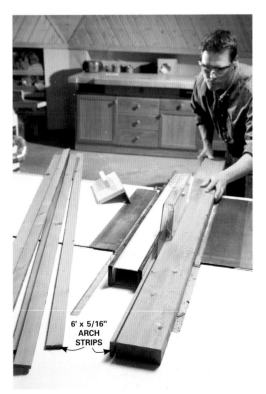

6' x 5/16" ARCH STRIPS

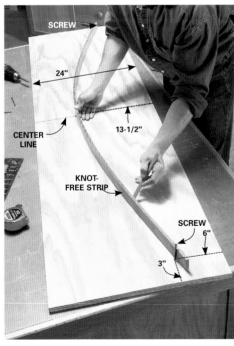

SCREW
24"
13-1/2"
CENTER LINE
KNOT-FREE STRIP
SCREW 6"
3"

2 Draw the arch on the bending jig plywood using one of the knot-free strips of wood and a pair of 3-in. screws.

Figure A Build the whole planter from two 8-ft.-long 2x8s

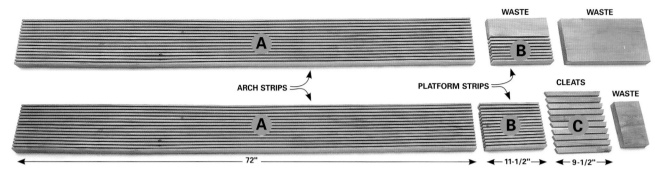

WASTE WASTE

A

B

ARCH STRIPS

PLATFORM STRIPS

CLEATS

WASTE

A

B C

72" 11-1/2" 9-1/2"

Cut the parts

Cut each 2x8 to the lengths called for in Figure A and
then start the ripping process. Ripping 5/16-in.-wide
strips can be hazardous, so be sure to use a push carriage
(Photo 1). Make your carriage from 1/4-in. and 3/4-in.
plywood, custom-sized to match the height of the table
saw fence. We were able to cut 15 strips from each board, but
you may get fewer depending on the thickness of your blade.
Don't worry if you wind up with fewer or unusable ones; you can
build each arch with as few as 13 strips. Just make sure to use the same
quantity for each arch so they'll match. If any of the strips break at knots,
keep the pieces together, because you can still use them (more on this later).

Rip the platform slats next and then the 1/2- x 3/4-in. platform cleats. Rip the
pieces first to 3/4 in. wide from a chunk of 2x8, then turn the 1-1/2-in. strips on their
sides and rip them into 1/2-in. strips. Cut the cleats to length with decorative 22-degree
angles on the ends.

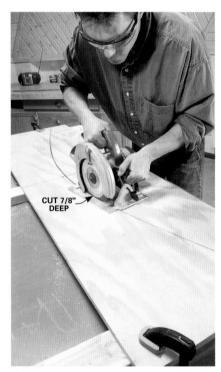

CUT 7/8"
DEEP

3 Set the blade of the circular saw to cut
7/8 in. deep and cut the curve. Clamp
the plywood to the workbench and hold your
saw with both hands.

GAP

3/4" SPACER

4 Clamp 15 strips in the bending jig and re-mark the top curve with a 3/4-in. spacer block.
Then remove the strips and recut that curve only.

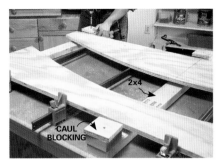

CAUL
BLOCKING

2x4

5 Screw together three clamping cauls, adding blocks as needed so they'll be even with the top of the laminating strips (see Photo 7).

Make the bending jig

Cut the plywood for the bending jig to size (Photo 2) and use one of the knot-free strips to form the curve. Use 3-in. screws partially driven into the plywood at the locations we show and push the center of the strip 13-1/2 in. out from the edge while you scribe the curve. Don't beat yourself up striving for a perfect curve; small variations won't be noticeable. It may seem odd to make this curved cut with a circular saw (Photo 3), but it's surprisingly easy and safe on a gentle curve like this. The curve will be smoother than any you can achieve with a jigsaw. Just make sure to set your blade depth at 7/8 in. Any deeper and the blade may bind and kick back.

The two curves on the two sections of the jig are slightly different, and you'll have to recut the top part of the jig to match the bottom. To find this difference, lay 15 strips in the jig and tighten the clamps until the arch is completely formed (Photo 4). You'll have to tighten the clamps in "turns" as the strips gradually bend; that is, tighten two clamps until they run out of threads. Then leave them in place while you completely unscrew the other two, slide those jaws tight to the jig and continue tightening those. Work on pairs, tightening the outer two, then the inner two. You'll get the feel for the clamping process on this "glue-less" dry run and it'll make the actual glue-up easier. When the clamps are tight, the strips will be tight to the jig at the bottom and there'll be a gap between the arch and the jig at the top. Trace around the top with a

EXTERIOR WOOD GLUE

MINI ROLLER

CENTER LINE MARK

PAINTER'S PLASTIC

6 Roll glue onto both sides of each strip (one side of top and bottom strips) and position them, keeping the jig and strip center lines aligned.

CAUL

7 Pull the jig together as far as possible and snug up the clamps. Then screw the cauls down and finish tightening the clamps.

3/4-in. spacer to re-mark the top curve (Photo 4). Then unclamp everything and recut that part of the jig.

Block up the cauls and glue up the arches

During glue-up, the strips have a tendency to lift away from the clamps while the glue is wet and slippery because

of the stresses in the curves. "Cauls" are simply blocks of wood that hold the strips flat and prevent this. Make the cauls from six 2x4s (three on both the bottom and the top) and space them evenly with blocking sized so the cauls will be flush with the top of the arch (Photo 7). Have these ready to go before the glue-up—you won't have time to spare later.

Mark a center line on the strips and

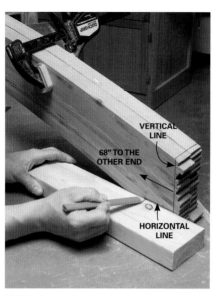

8 Remove the cauls after one hour and scrape off the excess glue from that side. Remove the clamps after three hours and scrape the glue from the other side.

9 Belt-sand both sides of the arch flat with 60-grit paper, then 80-grit. Smooth the surface with a random-orbital sander with 100-grit paper.

10 Clamp the arches together and draw vertical lines just short of the ends. Then scribe the bottom horizontal lines with a 2x4 spacer. Cut the ends with a circular saw.

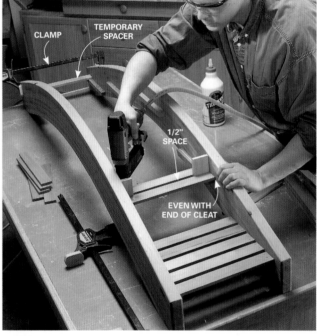

11 Lay the cleat-mounting template (Figure B) flush with the arch bottoms. Then glue and nail the end cleats. Rest the template over the first set of cleats and mount the next two cleats, then move it again to mount the top cleat.

12 Space and clamp the arches. Then glue and nail the platform strips on the cleats, keeping them even with the cleat ends and spacing them 1/2 in. apart.

keep them aligned with the bending jig center line when you start gluing later (Photo 6). Lay painter's plastic directly below the jig to keep your workbench and clamps clean and then start gluing the strips. A mini paint roller greatly speeds up the process, and time is of the essence. Glue both sides of each strip and push the glued surfaces lightly together to delay glue setup. Slip in any broken strips near the middle of the arch, matching

up the breaks after they're coated with glue. Use flawless strips for the first and last strips of each arch. After you spread the glue, pull the jig together, bending the strips as far as you can while a helper slides the clamps closed. That'll speed up the clamping process. Then lay plastic over the caul locations, screw the cauls into place, screw the top 2x4s into place and tighten the clamps. Again, work on pairs, progressively tightening

Figure B Cleat template

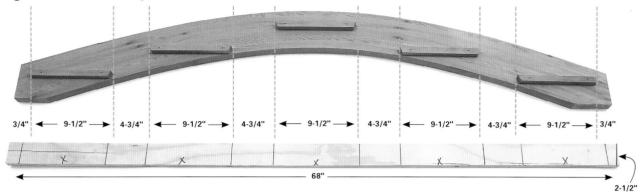

| 3/4" | 9-1/2" | 4-3/4" | 9-1/2" | 4-3/4" | 9-1/2" | 4-3/4" | 9-1/2" | 4-3/4" | 9-1/2" | 3/4" |

68"

2-1/2"

them. Work quickly. If you still see gaps between any strips, close them by driving a wedge between the jig and the arch or add more bar clamps from above. Ignore the clamping instructions on the glue bottle—leave the clamps in place for at least three hours.

You don't have to wait until you've removed the clamps to start cleaning up glue and flattening the arch. As the glue starts to "gel up" (dry to the touch but gooey beneath the surface, about one hour into clamping), remove the cauls (leave the clamps tightened) and start scraping away the glue from the top side of the arch. A paint scraper works great for most of it; use a small chisel or screwdriver to get into the crevices. The key is to remove as much glue as possible. Hardened glue is nearly impossible to remove and any leftover glue will clog and ruin sanding belts in no time. After you've scraped off the glue, wipe off any other glue smears with a damp (not wet!) rag. Don't worry about the bottom side yet; you can get it after the three-hour clamping period. The glue there will stay softer longer because it's against the plastic.

Flatten the arches and cut the ends

Start belt-sanding diagonally with 60-grit belts to knock off the high spots (Photo 9). After the surface is flat, remove cross-grain sanding marks by sanding following the curve. Then belt-sand with 80- and then 100-grit belts. Finish up with 100-grit paper in a random-orbital sander. Remove the arch from the jig, scrape off the glue, and flatten and sand the opposite side. Then repeat the whole process for the other arch.

If you have a benchtop planer, use it for the whole flattening process. Feed in one end and you'll be able to gently push the arch sideways and follow the curve as it goes through the machine. Make sure all the glue on the surface is removed. Hardened glue will dull the cutting knives.

Mark and cut off the bottom and ends as we show in Photo 10. Cut one end first, then measure over 68 in. and cut the other end. Ease the sharp edges of each arch with a round-over router bit or sandpaper.

Mount the cleats and the platforms

We show you an easy way to mount the cleats on both arches using a mounting template made from plywood (Photo 11 and Figure B). Cut it to 68 in. and lay out the cleat positions as shown. Then position and fasten the cleats (Photo 11).

Separate the arches with temporary platform strips and lightly clamp the arches together (Photo 12). Make sure the arch ends are even, then glue and nail the platforms to the cleats.

If you'd like a finish on your planter, use any stain designed for exterior siding. To further protect your planter against rot, spread exterior wood glue on the feet of each arch.

3 DECK & WINDOW PLANTERS

Sturdy deck planter

WHAT IT TAKES

TIME: 4 hours
SKILL LEVEL: Beginner

This easy-to-make flower box sits on almost any deck rail ... or can even stand alone

Looking for a planter box that fits in just about anywhere? Then this sturdy and attractive planter box is what you need.

Its clever design means it can rest securely on a 2x4 or 2x6 deck railing or sit on a patio, porch or deck floor without tipping. Plus, it can be made just about any length you want. If that's not enough to get you building, it's easy to make, even for first-time woodworkers. You won't need a boatload of tools, either. A table saw is a must, but if you don't have one, perhaps a neighbor or friend can help. Spend a few extra dollars on cedar, redwood or cypress. These woods hold up better to the moisture they'll face from watering flowers.

Figure A
Deck planter

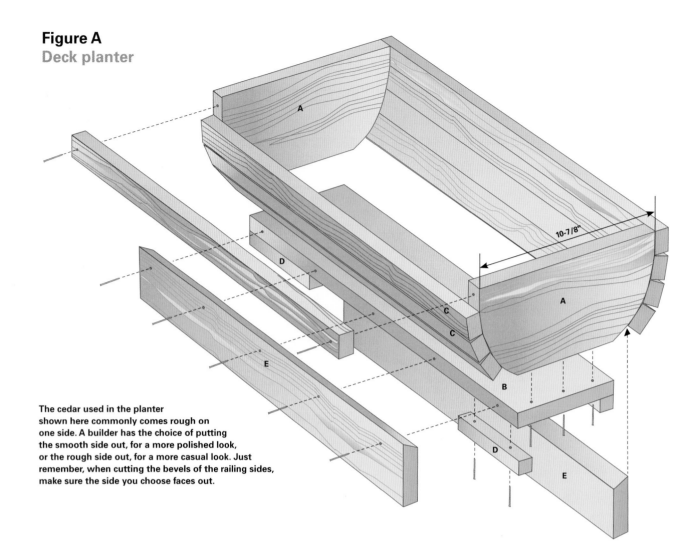

10-7/8"

The cedar used in the planter shown here commonly comes rough on one side. A builder has the choice of putting the smooth side out, for a more polished look, or the rough side out, for a more casual look. Just remember, when cutting the bevels of the railing sides, make sure the side you choose faces out.

Here's how to build it

Enlarge the end pattern (Figure B on p. 35) to exactly 10-7/8 in. Cut two boards to a length of 12 in. and tape or glue the patterns onto the boards. With a jigsaw or band saw, cut each end (A) using the pattern as a guide (Photo 1).

Mark the length of your box on the boards four times, for parts B, C and D, avoiding knots at the ends; cut to length. The planter box shown is 24 in. long.

On a table saw, cut the bottom board (B), slats (C) and railing spacers (D) to width. See the Cutting List.

Cut the railing sides (E), putting a 35-degree bevel along one edge. Be careful here—remember one side is rough and the other smooth. You can have either side facing out, but be sure to cut the angles the proper direction so the finish you prefer faces out.

Stand each end with the top edge down on your workbench and space them apart the length of the bottom board. Center the bottom board on each end and drill pilot holes to avoid splitting the wood. Use waterproof

Materials list

*	1x8 x 10' rough cedar, redwood or cypress (for 24" planter)
1 box	1-1/2" galvanized finishing nails
1 tube	Waterproof construction adhesive
1 qt.	Clear sealer or deck stain (optional)

*Quantity is determined by the length of your box

Cutting list

KEY	QTY.	SIZE & DESCRIPTION
A	2	Enlarge Figure B to 10-7/8" wide (ends)
B	1	5-5/8" x 24"* (bottom)
C	8	1-3/8" x 24"* (slats)
D	4	1" x 5-1/2" (spacers)
E	2	3-3/8" x 24"* (railing sides)

*Length should be adjusted equally on pieces B, C and E.

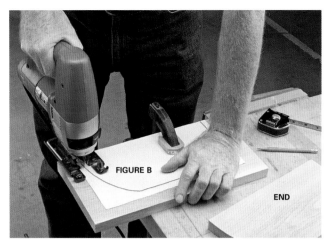

1 Cut out the ends using a jigsaw. Use a fine-tooth blade and follow the paper pattern attached to each end board with tape or glue.

2 Glue the joints so your deck planter will last for years. Before attaching the bottom to the ends, drill pilot holes first so that you don't split the wood when nailing.

3 Attach railing sides to the bottom. The beveled edge allows the sides to fit snugly against the curved bottom of each end.

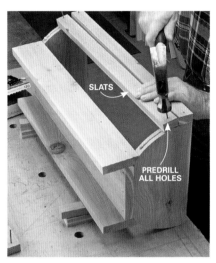

4 Nail side slats starting from the top of the box, working your way toward the bottom. Remember, pilot holes are a must when nailing close to the ends of these pieces.

5 Add rail spacers to the inside of each railing side. These clever additions allow this box to sit snugly atop a 2x6 or 2x4 railing.

Figure B End pattern

Enlarge approx. 400%, to 10-7/8". If drawing, use a 1" grid.

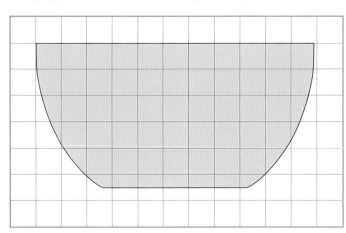

construction adhesive on all joints (Photo 2) before nailing pieces in place.

Nail the railing sides to the bottom as shown in Photo 3. The bevel fits the curve of the end boards nicely.

Working from the top to the bottom (Photo 4), predrill and attach the side slats on both sides of the box.

The spacers should be attached to the inside of each railing side as shown in Photo 5. These spacers strengthen the railing sides and also allow the box to snugly hold onto a 2x4 deck rail.

If you're applying a stain or sealer to help protect the wood, allow the adhesive to dry 24 hours.

In the meantime, go to the garden center for some potting soil and colorful flowers to brighten up your deck, patio or porch.

Stair-step plant display

WHAT IT TAKES

TIME: 4 hours
SKILL LEVEL: Beginner

Show off your favorite plants with this simple cedar stand.

We tend to buy plants first and worry about good spots for them later. So unfortunately, many of the prettiest plants get lost in the corners of a deck and sunroom and don't get the attention (or the light) they deserve.

To help solve this problem and to spotlight some favorite plants, we came up with this simple display stand. It's made from cedar 1x2s that are cut into just two lengths, stacked into squares and nailed together. We used western red cedar with the rough-sawn side exposed. Assembly is simple and fast, because there's nothing to measure as you build—just keep everything square and use the wood pieces themselves for spacing and alignment.

Here's what you'll need

For supplies, you'll need seven 8-ft.-long cedar 1x2s, exterior glue, a few dozen 4d galvanized finish nails, and some 100- or 120-grit sandpaper. You'll also need a hammer, a tape measure and a framing square, plus a saw that can cut the 1x2s to a consistent length. A power miter saw is great for this (you can rent one) but you could also use a handsaw in a miter box. An exterior finish for the wood is attractive, but not really necessary.

Begin by trimming any rough or out-of-square ends from your 1x2s. Almost all the ends will show, so they need to look good. Cut the 1x2s into sixteen 20-in. pieces and twenty-seven 10-3/4-in. pieces. It's important that the two groups of pieces are consistent in length, so rather than measuring each one, clamp a "stop block" to your bench the appropriate distance from the blade of your saw, and push the 1x2 up against it for each cut.

How to build it

Begin making your stand by arranging the lowest two layers without nails or glue (Photo 1). Lay out the bottom three 20-in. pieces against a framing square,

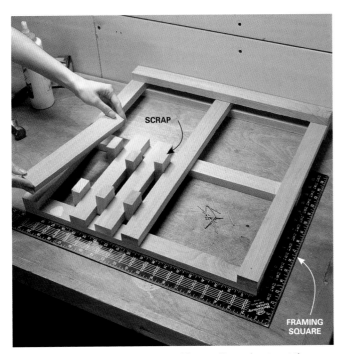

1 Assemble the first two layers without nails or glue to get the spacing right and to make sure everything is square. Use scrap pieces of 1x2 as spacers. Once everything is square, glue and nail all the intersections.

SCRAP

FRAMING SQUARE

2 Build up the stand "log-cabin style" until you get to the seventh layer, which has two platforms. When that's nailed down, continue until the 12th layer, which has the final platform.

SEVENTH LAYER

then lay three more 20-in. pieces and three 10-3/4-in. pieces on top of them as shown in Photo 1.

Adjust the spacing, using scrap pieces to create the gaps, and make sure everything is square. The second layer should have a plant platform in one corner and nothing in the other three. When everything looks good, nail the pieces together, using one nail and a dab of glue at every intersection. Keep the nails 3/4 in. away from the ends of the boards to prevent splitting.

Add five more layers each consisting of two long and one short piece, with glue and a nail at every overlap. Check the sides with the square as you go to keep them straight. At the seventh layer, add two more platforms, with the 10-3/4-in. pieces running perpendicular to the pieces on the first platform. Add another five layers, with just two 10-3/4-in. pieces per layer, then fill in the top layer to create the final display platform (Photo 2). When you're done nailing, sand all the outside edges of your stand and apply an exterior stain or preservative. Wait a few days for the finish to dry completely, then start moving in the plants!

Tip

Always nail at least 3/4 in. in from the end, and if the wood still splits, predrill the nail holes using a bit the size of the nail or the nail itself with the head snipped off. Your boards may also differ in thickness from those shown, which were 13/16 in. thick. If so, simply adjust the spacing between the boards.

Figure A
Exploded view

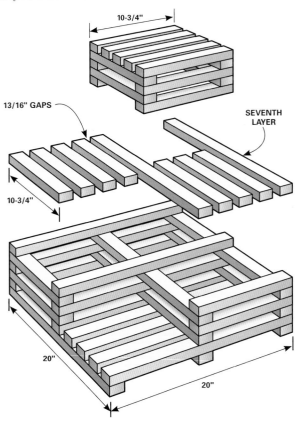

10-3/4"

13/16" GAPS

10-3/4"

SEVENTH LAYER

20"

20"

Patio planters

Build them any size and give your potted plants a simple, stylish home— outdoors or in

This planter is designed to make your patio or deck gardening much easier. Instead of filling it with dirt and planting each flower or plant individually, you simply set prepotted plants right into the planter. You can conveniently switch plants as the season changes or unload the planter and move it to a new location.

We designed this project to fit any pot with an 11-in. diameter or less and a maximum height of 10-1/2 in. To create the illusion of a fully planted box, you just fill in around the pots with wood chips, bark or other mulch covering. The base or bottom of the planter has 7/8-in. holes drilled every 6 in. to drain away any excess water. The side boards have a 1/4-in. space between them to ventilate the mulch and keep it from getting soggy.

WHAT IT TAKES

TIME: 1 day
SKILL LEVEL: Intermediate

Figure A
Leg template
(enlarge 400%)

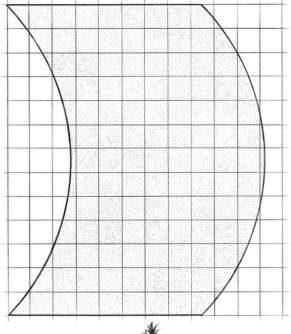

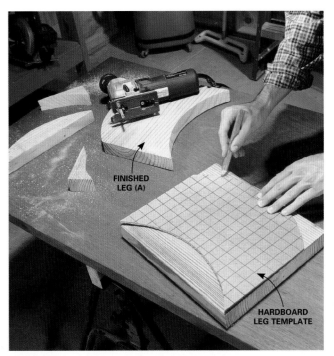

FINISHED
LEG (A)

HARDBOARD
LEG TEMPLATE

1 Using a full-size template made from Figure A, trace the outline of the planter legs onto pressure-treated 2x12 pine boards. Sand the edges with a finish or belt sander followed by 100-grit hand-sanding to gently ease the edges.

Cutting list for large planter

KEY	QTY.	SIZE & DESCRIPTION
A	4	1-1/2" x 11-1/4" x 13" treated pine legs
B	1	1-1/2" x 11-1/4" x 48" treated pine base
C	4	1-1/2" x 5-1/2" x 48" cedar side panels
D	4	1-1/2" x 5-1/2" x 14-1/4" cedar end panels*
E	2	1-1/16" x 4-1/2" x 57" cedar side aprons
F	2	1-1/16" x 4-1/2" x 20-1/4" cedar side aprons*

Cutting list for small planter

KEY	QTY.	SIZE & DESCRIPTION
A	4	1-1/2" x 11-1/4" x 13" treated pine legs
B	1	1-1/2" x 11-1/4" x 36" treated pine base
C	4	1-1/2" x 5-1/2" x 36" cedar side panels
D	4	1-1/2" x 5-1/2" x 14-1/4" cedar end panels*
E	2	1-1/16" x 4-1/2" x 45" cedar side aprons
F	2	1-1/16" x 4-1/2" x 20-1/4" cedar side aprons*

*Cut to fit

12" SPEED
SQUARE

SUPPORT
BLOCK

2 Make straight cuts using a 12-in. Speed square held firmly against the back of the 2x6.

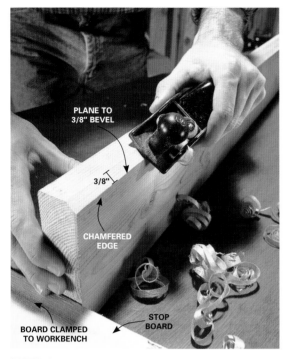

PLANE TO
3/8" BEVEL

3/8"

CHAMFERED
EDGE

BOARD CLAMPED
TO WORKBENCH

STOP
BOARD

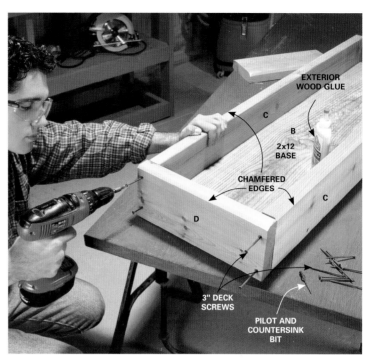

EXTERIOR
WOOD GLUE

C

B

2x12
BASE

CHAMFERED
EDGES

C

D

3" DECK
SCREWS

PILOT AND
COUNTERSINK
BIT

3 Plane only the edges where the side boards C and D meet. This chamfered edge should be about 3/8 in. wide when completed. Clamp a board to the edge of your workbench to stop the workpiece from drifting while you stroke the edge of the board with the plane.

4 Cut your 2x12 base to length, then screw the lower sides (C) to the base. Align the base and sides so they're flush on the bottom sides. Predrill for each screw using a pilot/countersink combination bit. Then screw the ends to the sides.

CLAMP

C

2-1/2" DECK
SCREWS

A

LEAVE 3/16"
TO EDGE

D

SHIMS

5 Shim the base up 1-3/4 in. on each side using scrap pieces of wood, then clamp the legs one at a time to the sides (C). Screw the sides to the legs with 2-1/2 in. deck screws. Use three screws per leg.

We've shown you two planters of different lengths, but you can adapt them to fit your unique space. You can even change the width by nailing a treated 2x2 to the side of the 2x12 base piece to accommodate a slightly wider pot. To build either the small or large planter shown, follow our clear step-by-step photos and refer to the Cutting List for lumber lengths.

Buying the right lumber

You'll notice the legs are treated pine and not cedar like the sides and top apron. Treated pine is less likely to split along the grain (a nasty problem with cedar). Pick treated 2x12 material for the legs with as few large knots as possible. You'll be able to cut around knots on a single board, so bring a tape measure when you select the lumber. Choose straight cedar for the sides and remember that some knots here can add to the overall beauty.

Feel free to use other species of wood such as redwood, cypress or even a plantation-grown tropical wood like ipe (available at some lumberyards).

DRILL 7/8"
DRAIN HOLES
EVERY 6"

6 Clamp the upper sides flush to the tops of the legs. Be sure to align the upper and lower side ends before drilling and screwing this piece in place. Again, use three 2-1/2 in. deck screws per leg. Next, screw the upper end panels (D) to the upper sides. Make sure the chamfers face each other on each side.

Use paint, stain or a combination of both

We chose an exterior enamel paint for the legs and apron pieces to accent the deck oil stain/sealer on the base and sides. Stain is a better choice than paint for the base and sides because they'll be exposed to more moisture than the legs and top. The photo below shows the excellent results you can get by staining the entire project with an exterior oil deck stain.

5/4 x 6
CEDAR DECK
BOARD

7 Rip the 5/4 x 6 deck boards to 4-1/2 in. to make the top apron frame. Use a rip guide on your circular saw or a table saw if you have one. Plane and sand the cut edge to match the factory-machined edge of the deck board.

6d GALVANIZED
CASING NAILS

8 Glue and nail the side apron pieces (E) flush with parts C below. Next, nail the apron end pieces to the end panels (D). You'll notice the inside edge of F will be about 1/4 in. out from the inside of the planter to adequately cover the tops of the legs.

Rot-proof window-planter

WHAT IT TAKES

TIME: 2 hours
SKILL LEVEL: Beginner

You can't beat the look of a real wood window box on a home. Wood takes paint well, so you can tailor the box's color scheme to complement your house. But ordinary wooden boxes rot out in just a few

years, and plastic window boxes won't rot but don't look as nice as the traditional wood box.

This window box design incorporates the best of both materials. Buy a plastic window box at a home or garden center, then construct a cedar frame around it. Size the frame so the lip of the plastic window box rests on the wood. There's no need for a bottom. Cut the front side of each end piece at a 5-degree angle, then screw together the frame with 2-in. deck screws. Attach the box to the house with a pair of L-brackets, and you're ready to get growing.

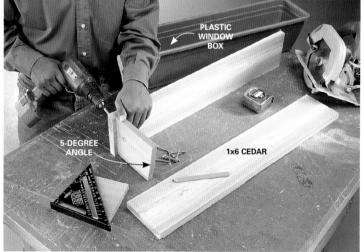

PLASTIC WINDOW BOX

5-DEGREE ANGLE

1x6 CEDAR

4 BENCHES

3-hour cedar bench

Materials list

QTY.	ITEM
2	1x3 x 8' cedar
1	2x10 x 8' cedar
5	2x4 x 8' cedar
1 lb.	3" deck screws
1/4 lb.	6d galv. casing nails
2	3/8" x 5" bolts with nuts and washers

WHAT IT TAKES

TIME: 3 hours
SKILL LEVEL: Beginner to intermediate

Build it in an afternoon!

The beauty of this cedar bench isn't just that it's easy to assemble and inexpensive—it's that it's so doggone comfortable. You can comfortably sit on your custom-fit bench for hours, even without cushions. Here, you'll learn how to build the bench and how to adjust it for maximum comfort.

Sloping the back and the seat is the secret to pain-free perching on unpadded flat boards. But not all bodies are the same, and it's a rare piece of furniture that everyone agrees is seatworthy. This bench has a bolted pivot point where the back and the seat meet that lets you alter the backrest and seat slopes to fit your build during one of the final assembly steps (Photo 10). Cutting all the parts and assembling them will only take about three hours. Follow the step-by-step photo series for details on the simple construction.

Figure A
Bench parts

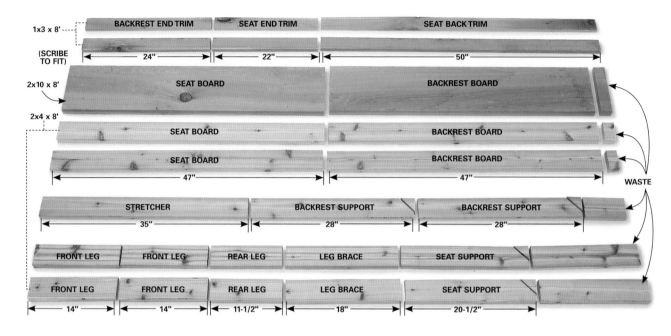

1x3 x 8' ----
(SCRIBE TO FIT)

| BACKREST END TRIM | SEAT END TRIM | SEAT BACK TRIM |
| 24" | 22" | 50" |

2x10 x 8'

| SEAT BOARD | BACKREST BOARD | WASTE |

2x4 x 8'

SEAT BOARD	BACKREST BOARD
SEAT BOARD	BACKREST BOARD
47"	47"

| STRETCHER | BACKREST SUPPORT | BACKREST SUPPORT |
| 35" | 28" | 28" |

FRONT LEG	FRONT LEG	REAR LEG	LEG BRACE	SEAT SUPPORT
FRONT LEG	FRONT LEG	REAR LEG	LEG BRACE	SEAT SUPPORT
14"	14"	11-1/2"	18"	20-1/2"

Build it from eight 8-ft.-long boards and a handful of fasteners

A circular saw and a screw gun are the only power tools you really need for construction, although a power miter saw will speed things up and give you cleaner cuts. Begin by cutting the boards to length. Figure A shows you how to cut up the eight boards efficiently, leaving little waste. When you're picking out the wood at the lumberyard, choose boards that above all are flat, not twisted. That's especially important for the seat and back parts. Don't worry so much about the leg assembly 2x4s because you cut them into such short pieces that warps and twists aren't much of a concern.

After cutting the pieces to length, screw together the leg assemblies (Photos 2 – 6). It's important to use a square to keep the leg braces square to the legs (Photo 2). That way both leg assemblies will be identical and the bench won't wobble if it's put on a hard, flat surface. The leg brace is spaced 1/2 in. back from the front of the legs to create a more attractive shadow line. Then it's just a matter of connecting the leg assemblies with the stretcher (Photo 7), screwing down the seat and backrest boards, and adjusting the slopes to fit your body.

The easiest way to adjust the slope is to hold the four locking points in place with clamps and then back out the temporary screws (Photo 10). To customize the slopes, you just loosen the clamps, make the

GUIDE SQUARE

1 Cut out the bench parts following the measurements in Figure A. Use a square to guide the circular saw for accurate, square cuts. Cut 45-degree angles on the ends of the seat and back supports 1 in. down from the ends as shown (also see Photos 4 and 5).

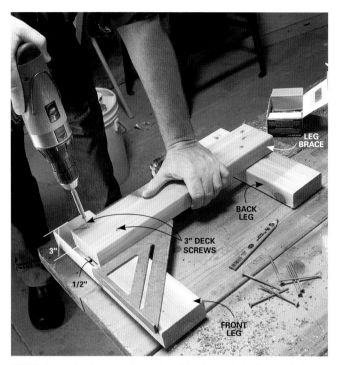

2 Fasten the leg brace to the legs 3 in. above the bottom ends. Angle the 3-in. screws slightly to prevent the screw tips from protruding through the other side. Hold the brace 1/2 in. back from the front edge of the front leg. Use a square to make sure the brace and legs are at exact right angles.

3 Align the second part of the front leg with the first one using a square and screw it to the leg brace as shown.

4 Slip the seat support between the two front legs, positioning it as shown. Drive a single 3-in. screw through the front leg into the seat support.

5 Position the backrest support on the leg assembly as shown, making sure it's at a right angle with the seat support, and mark the position on the seat support. Then drive a 3-in. screw through the middle of the backrest support into the leg brace.

6 Clamp the backrest support, seat support and rear leg as shown using the line as a guide. Drill a 3/8-in. hole through the center of the assembly. Drive a 3/8-in. x 5-in. bolt fitted with a washer through the hole and slightly tighten the nut against a washer on the other side.

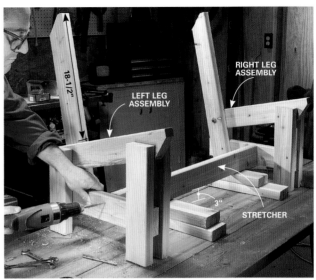

7 Assemble the other leg assembly to *mirror* the first as shown. (The back support and rear leg switch sides.) Prop the stretcher 3 in. above the workbench, center it between the front and rear bench legs and screw the leg braces into the ends with two 3-in. deck screws.

adjustments, retighten and test the fit. When you're satisfied, run a couple of permanent screws into each joint. If you don't have clamps, don't worry—you'll just have to back out the screws, adjust the slopes, reset the screws and test the bench. Clamps just speed up the process.

Round over the edges

We show an option of rounding over the sharp edge of the 1x3 trim, which is best done with a router and a 1/2-in. round-over bit (Photo 12). Rounding over the edges can protect shins and the backs of thighs and leave teetering toddlers with goose eggs on their melons instead of gashes. So the step is highly recommended. If you don't have a router, round over the edge either by hand-sanding or with an orbital or belt sander. In any event, keep the casing nails 1 in. away from the edge to prevent hitting the nailheads with the router bit or sandpaper (Photo 12).

Building a longer bench

We demonstrate how to build a 4-ft.-long bench, plenty of space for two. But you can use the same design and techniques for building 6- or 8-ft. long benches too. You'll just have to buy longer boards for the seat, back, stretcher and the trim boards. While you're at it, you can use the same design for matching end or coffee tables. Just match the double front leg design for the rear legs, and build flat-topped leg assemblies with an overall depth of 16-3/4 in.

Seal the legs to make it last

If you want to stain your bench, use a latex exterior stain on the parts after cutting them to length. After assembly, you won't be able to get good penetration at the cracks and crevices. Avoid clear exterior sealers, which will irritate bare skin. But

8 Center the first 2x4 seat board over the leg assemblies and flush with the front ends of the seat supports. Screw it to the seat supports with two 3-in. deck screws spaced about 1 in. away from the edges. Line up the 2x10 with the first 2x4, space it about 5/16 in. away (the thickness of a carpenter's pencil) and screw it to the seat supports with two 3-in. deck screws. Repeat with the rear 2x4.

Tip

If you want to save a few bucks—or if cedar is difficult to find in your area—you can build this bench from pressure-treated lumber. Just make sure the boards are relatively dry and don't contain too many large knots.

9 Rest the bottom backrest 2x4 on carpenter's pencils, holding the end flush with the seat boards and screw it to the seat back braces. Then space and screw on the center 2x10 and the top 2x4 backrest boards.

10 Sit on the bench and decide if you'd like to tilt the seat or the backrest or both to make the bench more comfortable. To make seat or back adjustments, loosen the bolts and clamp the bottoms of the seat back supports and the fronts of the seat supports. Then back out the four screws at those points. Loosen the clamps, make adjustments, then retighten and retest for comfort. When you're satisfied with the fit, drive in the four original screws plus another at each point. Retighten the pivot bolts.

11 Tack the seat trim boards to the seat with the ends flush with the front and top. Scribe and cut the trim boards to fit. Nail the boards to the seat and backrest boards with 6d galvanized casing nails, keeping the nails 1 in. back from the seat edges.

12 Ease the edges of the trim boards with a router and a 1/2-in. round-over bit. Hold the router sideways to get at the seat/back corner.

the bench will last outside for more than 20 years without any stain or special care even if you decide to let it weather to a natural gray. However, the legs won't last that long because the end grain at the bottom will wick up moisture from the ground, making the legs rot long before the bench does. To make sure the legs last as long as the bench, seal the ends with epoxy, urethane or exterior woodworker's glue when you're through with the assembly.

Tip

You can use the same design and techniques for building a 4-, 6- or 8-foot-long bench.

North woods bench

An inexpensive, easy-to-build classic

The cute red stool shown below was made by an anonymous carpenter, and it's simplicity itself: pine boards, nailed together. It also has an interesting and ingenious design detail: a cloverleaf, clearly made with three overlapping drill holes. It's just the kind of little bench that's perfect for the backyard, so we went into the shop and made this modern version. A little longer and a little stronger than the original, but the same folk art detail. And since it's made from lumberyard pine, the price can't be beat. Here's how to make one.

This bench is simple enough to build with a few hand tools, but to speed things up, we chose to take advantage of the power tools in our shop. We used a miter saw to cut the stretchers to length and to cut the 10-degree angles on the ends of the center stretcher, and a circular saw for all the other cuts. If you don't own a miter saw, you can use a circular saw or jigsaw for all the cuts.

To make the holes for the clover shapes, you'll need a 1-in. hole saw mounted in a corded drill, or a powerful cordless drill.

We used No. 2 knotty pine to build this bench. You'll need one 6-ft. 1x12 and one 10-ft. 1x4. Select boards that are straight and flat, with solid, not loose, knots. We assembled the bench with countersunk 2-in. trim screws and then filled the holes with wood filler. If the bench is going outdoors, be sure to use corrosion-resistant screws.

Cut out the parts

Using the Cutting List, p. 53 as a guide, cut the two legs and the top from the 1x12 (Photo 1). The legs require a 10-degree bevel on the top and bottom. Be careful to keep both bevels angled the same direction. Then cut the stretcher and aprons to length. The stretcher has a 10-degree angle on each end.

Next, mark the legs and aprons for drilling and cutting, using the dimensions in Figures B and C as a guide. Draw the grid layout as shown in Photo 2 to locate the holes. Use a nail or a punch to make starting holes for the hole saw at the correct intersections.

1 Cut the leg blanks. Set the saw to cut a 10-degree bevel. Mark the 1x12 and align the saw with the mark. Then use a large square to help guide the cut.

10-DEGREE BEVEL

2 Drill out the clover shape. Mark out a grid with lines spaced 1/2 in. apart. The centers of the holes are on four of the intersections. Drill all four holes halfway through the board. Then flip the board over and drill from the other side to complete the holes.

1" HOLE SAW

1/2"
1/2"

3 Cut the leg angles. Mark the "V" in the center and the two outside angles on the legs. Then cut along the lines with a circular saw. Accurate cutting is easier if you clamp the leg to the workbench.

4 **Screw the aprons to the legs.** Drive trim screws through the legs into the stretcher. Then attach the outside aprons with trim screws.

TRIM SCREW

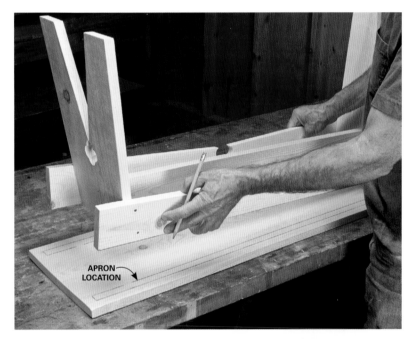

APRON LOCATION

5 **Position the seat screws.** Here's a goof-proof way to position the screws that fasten the seat to the bench frame. Center the frame on the seat and trace around the aprons. Then drill pilot holes through the seat to mark screw locations. Drive screws through the seat and into the aprons.

DRILL PILOT HOLE

Drill the 1-in. holes halfway through the boards (Photo 2). Make sure the pilot bit on the hole saw goes through the board so you can use the hole to guide the hole saw from the opposite side. Then flip the boards over to complete the holes.

Make the remaining cuts on the legs and aprons with a circular saw (Photo 3). Finish up by sanding the parts. We wrapped 80-grit sandpaper around a 1-in. dowel to sand the inside of the holes. Sand off the saw marks and round all the sharp edges slightly with sandpaper. If you plan to paint the bench, you can save time by painting the parts before assembly.

Build the bench

Start by marking the location of the stretcher on the legs. Arrange the legs so the bevels are oriented correctly, and screw through them into the stretcher. Next screw the two aprons to the legs (Photo 4).

The only thing left is to screw the top to the aprons. It'll be easier to place the screws accurately if you first mark the apron locations on the underside of the top and drill pilot holes for the screws (Photo 5). Stand the bench upright and align the top by looking underneath and lining up the apron marks. Then attach the top with six trim screws.

We finished this bench with old-fashioned milk paint. You can find milk paint online and at some paint stores. If the bench is going outdoors, rub some exterior glue on the bottom ends of the legs. That will prevent the end grain from soaking up moisture and rotting.

Figure A Exploded view

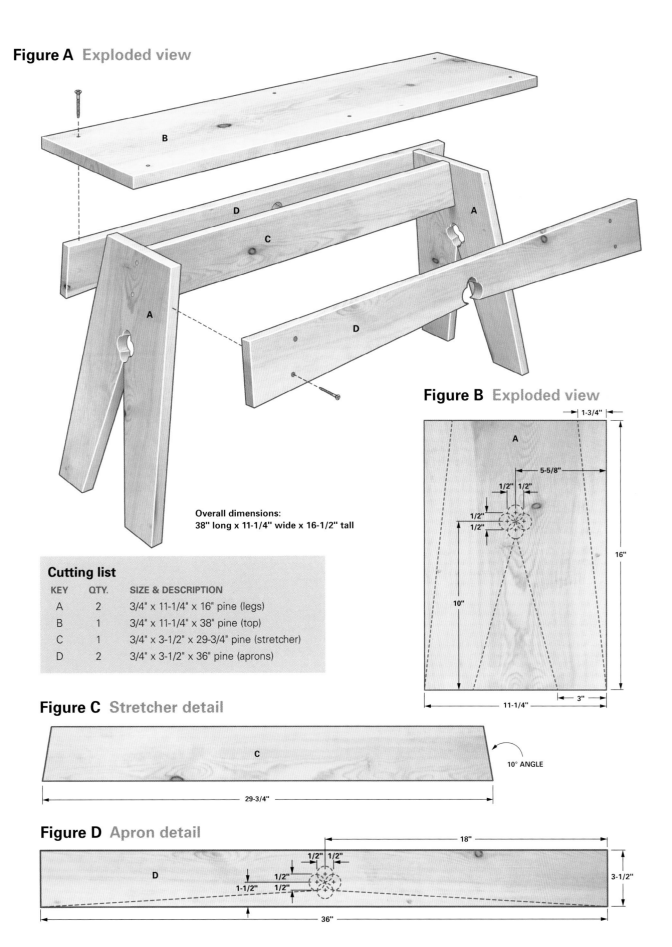

B

D

A

C

A

D

Overall dimensions:
38" long x 11-1/4" wide x 16-1/2" tall

Cutting list

KEY	QTY.	SIZE & DESCRIPTION
A	2	3/4" x 11-1/4" x 16" pine (legs)
B	1	3/4" x 11-1/4" x 38" pine (top)
C	1	3/4" x 3-1/2" x 29-3/4" pine (stretcher)
D	2	3/4" x 3-1/2" x 36" pine (aprons)

Figure B Exploded view

1-3/4"

A

5-5/8"

1/2" 1/2"

1/2"

1/2"

16"

10"

3"

11-1/4"

Figure C Stretcher detail

C

10° ANGLE

29-3/4"

Figure D Apron detail

18"

1/2" 1/2"

1/2"

3-1/2"

1-1/2" 1/2"

D

36"

Simplest bench in the world

WHAT IT TAKES

TIME: 2 hours
SKILL LEVEL: Beginner

Build it with a few 2x8s and a handful of screws

One of the easiest ways to make a good garden even better is to set a comfortable bench in a secluded corner. Just having a place to sit transforms an ordinary patch of flowers into a quiet contemplative refuge.

So if you're looking for a simple bench, take a look at this one, based on a design by Aldo Leopold, whom many consider the father of wildlife ecology.

Leopold's writings have led many to discover what it means to live in harmony with the land. If this bench was good enough for him, it's definitely good enough for the rest of us!

A little research led to this sturdy design which can be built quickly with a few 2x8s, glue and screws. Best of all, it's amazingly comfortable, perfect for bird-watching—even for two people.

1 Mark one end of the 2x8 x 10 at a 22-1/2-degree angle with a speed square or protractor, then cut with a circular saw. Make a mark 36 in. away and repeat the cut at the same angle. Cut the remaining front leg and two back legs from the same piece. Cut the seat and the backrest from the 2x8 x 8.

2 Fasten the legs together. Stack and clamp the seat and backrest to the edge of the worktable as guides, and then align the legs against them. Spread adhesive on the front leg, set the rear leg in place, and fasten the legs together with three 2-1/2-in. screws.

Building tips

To make a simple project even simpler, remember these tips:

- Be sure to assemble the legs (Step 2) so they're mirror images of each other, and not facing the same direction.
- Use clamps or a helper to hold the legs upright when securing the seat.
- Predrill all your screw holes to prevent splitting the wood.

Tools

Speed square or protractor

Drill with #8 countersink drill bit

Circular saw

Caulking gun

Materials list

1   2x8 x 8' cedar, redwood or treated lumber (seat and backrest)

1   2x8 x 10' cedar, redwood or treated lumber (front and rear legs)

Exterior construction adhesive

2-1/2" galvanized deck screws

3 Attach the seat and backrest. Stand the two ends up, 42 in. apart, spread glue on the tops of the rear legs, and screw the seat in place. Lay the bench on the worktable and attach the backrest with glue and screws.

Garden bench

WHAT IT TAKES

TIME: 1–2 days
SKILL LEVEL: Beginner to intermediate

A curved seat makes it comfortable; biscuit joinery makes it simple, strong

The first thing people notice about this bench is the design—simple but handsome. Then, as soon they sit down, they're all surprised by how comfortable it is.

This bench is just plain easy to build. It uses only biscuits and screws—the simplest types of joinery. Still, the bench is surprisingly strong. This one has been hauled around, knocked around and used as a mini scaffold—and once it even fell out of a moving pickup. But it's still solid.

Round up the tools and materials

You may have to buy more lumber than what it says in the Materials List, p. 58, to get knot-free pieces. You'll find everything you need to build this bench at your local home center or lumberyard. Refer to the Materials List; then choose the lumber carefully to avoid large knots.

In addition to the lumber, screws and wood plugs, you'll need No. 20 wood biscuits and a special tool called a plate or biscuit joiner to cut the biscuit slots. You can buy a good-quality biscuit joiner at any home center or online. You'll also need some clamps, a table saw and a router fitted with a 1/4-in. round-over bit.

1 Drill plug recesses.
Use a 1/2-in. Forstner bit to drill recesses for the screws. Later you'll fill them with wood plugs to hide the screws. You can easily control the depth of the hole by drilling until the top of the cutter is flush with the surface.

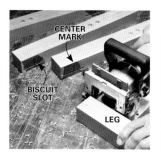

2 Cut biscuit slots for the seat rails.
Mark the centers of the biscuit slots on masking tape. Then, with the plug recesses facing up, cut the slots in the narrow sides of the legs. Keep the plate joiner and leg tight to the bench top as you cut. Use tape to avoid marks on the wood and to keep track of the orientation of the pieces.

3 Position slots for the long rails with a spacer.
Orient the leg so the previously cut slot is facing up, and cut a slot on the side opposite the plug holes. Use a spacer to position the slot so the long rail will be centered on the leg when it's installed.

Cut, drill and slot the parts

Start by inspecting your boards and planning the cuts to take advantage of the knot-free sections. Use a table saw to rip the boards to the right width. For crisp, clean edges, rip about 1/4 in. from the edge of the boards before you rip them to the final width. To work around knots, you may have to rough-cut some of the boards to approximate length before ripping them. When you're done ripping, cut the parts to length. We used a 1/4-in. round-over bit and router to ease the edges of the seat boards. It's a great task for a router table setup if you have one.

Next, measure and mark the center of all the screw holes and drill 3/8-in.-deep holes for the 1/2-in. wood plugs. We used a Forstner bit to create clean, flat-bottom holes. The final step in preparing the parts for assembly is cutting the biscuit slots. Rather than use the adjustable fence to position the slots, simply place your workpiece and the base of the biscuit joiner against the bench top and cut the slot.

4 Cut slots in the rail ends.
Mark the centers of the curved seat rails and long rails on masking tape. The tape also helps you keep track of the orientation of the slots.

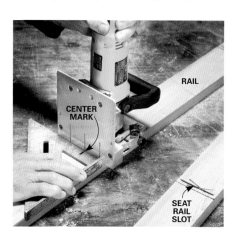

5 Cut slots in the long rails.
Position the long rails with the masking tape facing down. Use a Speed Square as a guide for cutting biscuit slots for the intermediate rails. Align the square with the edge mark for the seat rail. Make a center mark on the square as a reference for lining up the plate joiner.

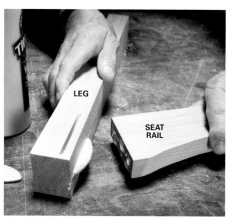

6 Join the seat rails and legs with biscuits.
Put a biscuit in the slot and dry-fit the leg and seat rail to make sure the rail is oriented correctly. It should be centered on the leg. Then spread glue in the slots and on the biscuit and press the leg and the seat rail together.

Figure A
Garden bench

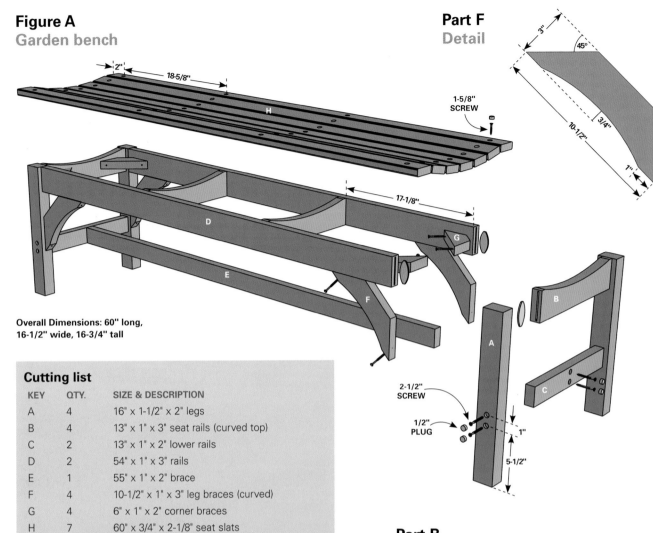

Overall Dimensions: 60" long,
16-1/2" wide, 16-3/4" tall

Part F
Detail

1-5/8"
SCREW

Part B
Detail

2-1/2"
SCREW

1/2"
PLUG

Cutting list

KEY	QTY.	SIZE & DESCRIPTION
A	4	16" x 1-1/2" x 2" legs
B	4	13" x 1" x 3" seat rails (curved top)
C	2	13" x 1" x 2" lower rails
D	2	54" x 1" x 3" rails
E	1	55" x 1" x 2" brace
F	4	10-1/2" x 1" x 3" leg braces (curved)
G	4	6" x 1" x 2" corner braces
H	7	60" x 3/4" x 2-1/8" seat slats

Materials list

ITEM	QTY.
2x4 x 8' cedar*	1
5/4x6 x 10' cedar decking*	2
1x6 x 6' cedar*	4
No. 20 biscuits	12
1-lb. box of 2-1/2" deck screws	1
1-lb. box of 1-5/8" deck screws	1
8-oz. bottle of exterior wood glue	1
1/2" flat-top wood plugs	40
Quart of exterior wood finish	1
*You may need extra if you want all knot-free parts.	

7 **Complete the leg assembly.** Use a spacer to support the lower rail. Then drive screws through the legs into the rail.

8 **Connect the seat rails with biscuits. Join** the two long rails with the two intermediate seat rails with biscuits and glue. Clamp them and let the glue set about 30 minutes.

Pay close attention to orientation as you cut the slots and assemble the bench. Use masking tape to keep track of the orientation. Photos 2 – 5 show the plate-joining techniques we used to cut slots in the parts.

Assemble the bench with biscuits and screws

Photos 6 – 11 show the assembly steps. Biscuits connect the legs to the rails for extra strength. Spread exterior wood glue in the slots and on the biscuits. Then clamp the parts until the glue sets. Use 2-1/2-in. deck screws to attach the legs to the braces (Photos 7 and 9). If you aren't using self-drilling screws, drill pilot holes to avoid splitting the parts. Attach the top slats to the frame with 1-5/8-in. deck screws. Plug the screw holes with 1/2-in. flat-top birch plugs. If you own a drill press, you can make your own cedar plugs using a 1/2-in. plug cutter.

We finished the bench with an exterior oil. This penetrating oil finish leaves the wood looking natural, but it has to be reapplied every year or two. For a glossy, more permanent finish, you could use spar varnish.

9 Join the leg and seat assemblies. Connect the leg assembies to the seat assembly with biscuits and clamp them together. Then attach the brace with screws.

10 Screw on the seat slats. Start by attaching the two outside slats. Then center the middle slat and attach it with screws. Next, position the remaining slats so there's an even space (two biscuits wide) between them. Use a board to align the slat ends.

11 Hide the screws with wood plugs. Glue flat-top wood plugs into the plug recesses. Use a cutoff dowel or a small block of wood to pound them flush.

5 GARDEN & DECK CHAIRS

Patio chair

The ultimate easy chair:
easy to build, easy to tote,
easy to set up and store.

Whether you're staking out a curbside spot for watching a parade, heading to the woods for a weekend or simply trying to catch a few rays, you'll love the portability and comfort of this chair. Interlocking legs and gravity keep the two sections together when in use. And when it's time to pull up stakes, the seat section tucks neatly inside the back. A handle cutout in the top slat makes for easy carrying and storing too.

WHAT IT TAKES

TIME: 8 hours for 1; 10 hours for 2
SKILL LEVEL: Intermediate

Getting started

We made our chair from cedar because it's lightweight, but you could use cypress, fir, treated or other decay-resistant woods. We didn't want knots weakening the legs or seat, so we spent extra for knot-free "D-grade" cedar, but you can find suitable pieces if you pick hrough the lumber piles. You'll need basic tools: a jigsaw, drill, Phillips bit, file, combination square, carpenter's square and screwdriver, plus a table saw and belt sander. If you don't own these last two tools, borrow them (or use this project as an excuse to add a few more tools to your workshop).

Building one chair takes about eight hours. But once you're "jigged up" and have your patterns made, building additional ones only takes an hour or two more each.

Make the patterns (by connecting the dots or with a photocopier)

The backrest and seat support struts must be the exact length and shape for the chair to set up and "nest" for storage properly. You can ensure accuracy two ways: You can place the strut grid (below) on a photocopier, then enlarge it until the squares are exactly 1 in. On our office machine, that meant first enlarging the grid 2x, taking that copy and enlarging it 2x, then taking that copy and enlarging it 1.30x. We taped two pieces of 8-1/2 x 11 paper together lengthwise to create the 18-in.-long pattern. Every copier is slightly different, so make sure the final grid is 18 in., and 18 squares, long. Then cut it out to create your pattern.

Materials list

2 pieces of 2x6 x 8' D and better-grade cedar (or equivalent)
2 pieces of 1x6 x 8' D and better-grade cedar
1 piece of 1/8" x 24" x 48" hardboard (for templates)
Eighty 2" galvanized deck screws
1 pint of exterior finish
Glue

Cutting list

KEY	PCS.	SIZE & DESCRIPTION
A	2	1-1/2" x 5-1/2" x 36" cedar (backrest struts)
B	2	1-1/2" x 4-15/16" x 34" cedar (seat struts)
C	1	3/4" x 4" x 20" cedar (top slat)
D	2	3/4" x 2-1/2" x 20" cedar (seat supports)
E	11	3/4" x 2" x 20" cedar (slats)

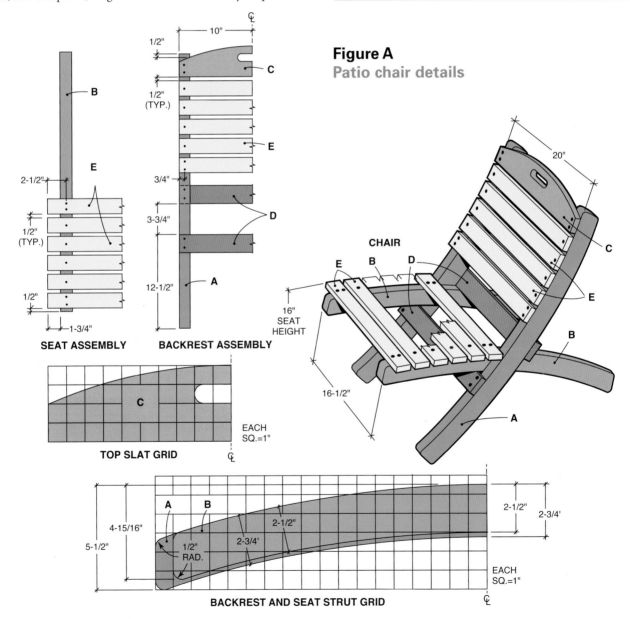

Figure A
Patio chair details

SEAT ASSEMBLY

BACKREST ASSEMBLY

CHAIR

TOP SLAT GRID

EACH SQ.=1"

BACKREST AND SEAT STRUT GRID

EACH SQ.=1"

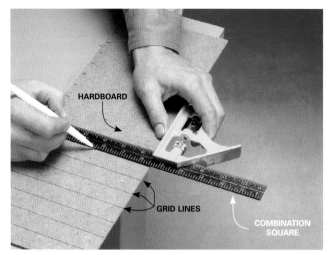

1 Measure and mark 1-in. increments on both ends and one side of the hardboard. Then draw grid lines using a combination square, straightedge and fine-point permanent marker. Or, if you like, you can use the photocopy method explained on p. 62.

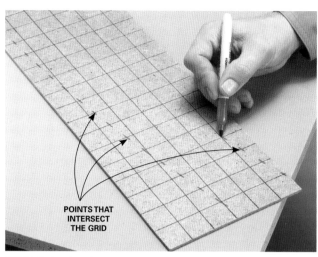

2 To develop the pattern, transfer the points to your hardboard grid where the shape intersects the grid lines in the drawing.

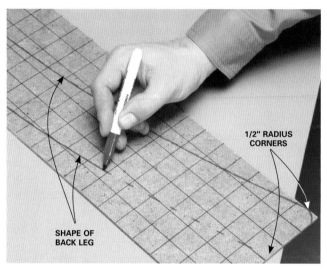

3 Draw lines connecting the points made on the grid. Use a smooth, arcing arm movement to draw the gradual curve. Use a quarter to trace the 1/2-in. radiuses at the bottom of the leg. Use a jigsaw to cut out the pattern.

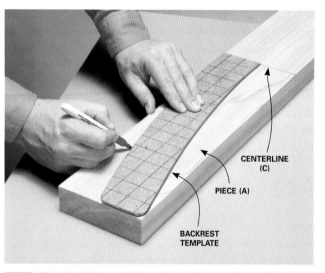

4 Align the backrest strut template to the centerline and bottom edge of the cedar piece and trace the shape. Flip the template along the centerline to draw the other half. Cut out the pieces with a jigsaw.

A second way is to use the transfer grid method (Photos 1 – 4). The shapes in Figure A are drawn on a scaled-down grid. Draw a full-size grid of 1-in. squares on hardboard (Photo 1) and transfer the shapes to it; you'll have a template you can use over and over.

We've drawn only half of the backrest and seat struts on our grids because the halves are symmetrical. Make one template for half of the shape, then flip it to draw the other half. Since the shapes of the seat and backrest struts are so similar, you can make only the backrest strut template, then use it to draw the seat strut pieces, making them 1/4 in. narrower and 1 in. shorter (2 in. shorter overall).

To use the template, align it to centerlines drawn on the boards (Photo 4), trace around it, then flip it over the centerline and trace the rest of the shape. Remember, the seat struts are 1/4 in. skinnier and 2 in. shorter than the backrest struts.

Putting it all together

Cut all the pieces to the dimensions given in the Cutting List, using the templates for the legs and the top slat. Cut out the shapes with a jigsaw, then sand the pieces with a belt sander (Photo 5). Lay out the hand grip hole in the top slat (C), then cut it out using a jigsaw and spade bit (Photo 6). You'll need to rip the back and seat slats 2 in. wide using a table saw.

Lay out, countersink and drill all the screw holes for the

Tip

Cedar is soft, so when screwing the pieces together, finish driving the screws by hand to avoid setting their heads too deep.

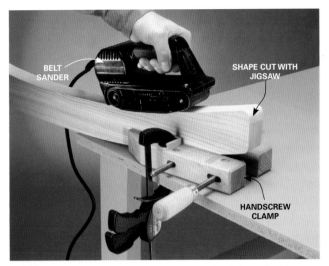

BELT SANDER

SHAPE CUT WITH JIGSAW

HANDSCREW CLAMP

5 Sand the edges of the curved pieces with a belt sander. If you don't have a bench vise, you can support the legs with a handscrew clamp while you sand.

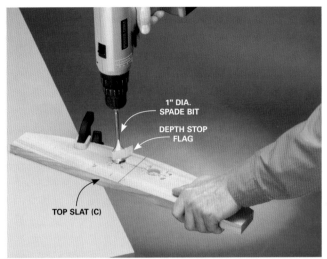

1" DIA. SPADE BIT

DEPTH STOP FLAG

TOP SLAT (C)

6 Drill the ends of the hand grip holes with a 1-in.-dia. spade bit. Drill partway in from both sides so you won't tear out the wood.

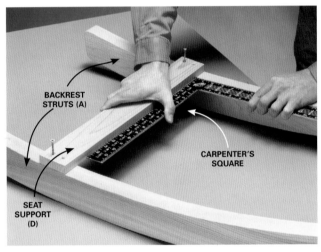

BACKREST STRUTS (A)

CARPENTER'S SQUARE

SEAT SUPPORT (D)

7 Use a carpenter's square to align the seat supports 90 degrees to the backrest struts, then glue and screw them in place. Use both glue and screws to attach the slats, too.

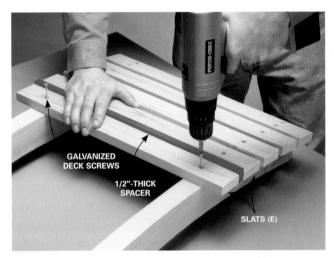

GALVANIZED DECK SCREWS

1/2"-THICK SPACER

SLATS (E)

8 Attach the slats to the seat struts using a 1/2-in.-thick spacer to align them. Finish driving the screws by hand to avoid setting their heads too deep.

slats and supports. Finish-sand all the pieces with 120-grit, then 150-grit sandpaper. Round over the sharp edges with the sandpaper.

Screw the two seat supports (D) and curved top slat to the backrest struts (Photo 7) using the spacing given in Figure A. Then attach the five slats to the backrest struts and six slats to the seat struts (Photo 8).

Finishing touches

Before applying the finish, unscrew the two seat supports and apply weather-resistant glue to the joints, then rescrew the seat supports to the backrest struts. The glue will strengthen the joint. The chair relies primarily on these seat supports for strength.

Brush on two liberal coats of a penetrating exterior wood sealer. Let the first coat dry for 24 hours, then apply the second coat. After an hour, wipe off any excess finish. Let the finish dry for a couple of days before using the chair. After a year or two, you'll want to recoat the chairs to keep them looking good. If you decide to paint the chairs instead, use an oil-based primer followed by a semigloss paint. Don't use a clear varnish; the sun will eventually break it down and you'll be refinishing every summer instead of relaxing.

Set up the chair by sliding the seat struts through the backrest struts and seat supports as shown in the photos on p. 61. Push the seat in all the way so the rear seat slat is firmly against the backrest struts. Then kick back and relax!

Yard & garden trio

WHAT IT TAKES

TIME: 2 weekends
SKILL LEVEL: Intermediate

A chair, love seat and table for your outdoor living room

At first glance, this trio of handcrafted outdoor furniture looks as if it's been part of the family for generations. The structure is solid and traditional, and the wood is stained a rich, weathered gray.

The carefully fitted joints give this chair, love seat and table the true look of furniture and not a stapled-together crate. Despite the refined look, they're not difficult to build. The construction-grade cedar parts are joined with dowels, glue, and screws hidden by wood plugs.

The knots and imperfections characteristic of lower grade cedar add to the furniture's charm. When you select your wood, however, be sure the knots are tight, the boards are straight, and there are no cracks to weaken the furniture.

To achieve the aged appearance, we brushed on a liberal coat of thinned-down gray deck stain (one part stain to two

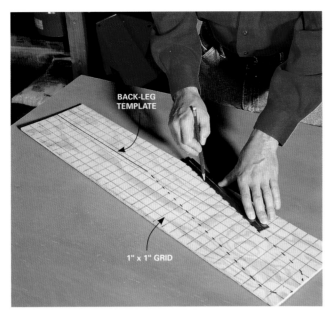

BACK-LEG
TEMPLATE

1" x 1" GRID

1 Make full-size templates for the shaped pieces. Transfer the intersecting points from our grid drawings to your full-size grids, then connect the points.

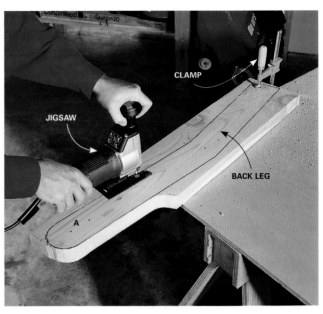

CLAMP

JIGSAW

BACK LEG

A

2 Cut out the shaped pieces using a jigsaw. Use a fine-tooth blade and carefully follow the drawn lines to reduce the amount of sanding needed to smooth the sawn edges.

parts mineral spirits). We continued brushing with the grain until the stain saturated the wood. To simulate wear, we brushed some areas even more to lighten the stain.

The three pieces should take you about two weekends to build. To simplify and speed up the cutting, we've provided templates for the shaped pieces that you can transfer to thin plywood.

Project background

The construction of all three pieces is very similar. We'll show you step-by-step how to build the chair; then you'll be able to build the love seat, which is essentially a longer version of the chair. One difference is the layout of the love seat's back top; see (B) in Figure A. Also, the love seat has an added center seat support (K) that's cut to fit between the back bottom and front seat supports (D). Glue and screw this extra piece in place just before attaching the seat slats (G). After making the chair and love seats, you'll find the table a snap (Figure B).

Make the chair templates

Gather all the tools plus your standard layout and carpentry tools. Using scrap

Cutting list

KEY	QTY.	SIZE	DESCRIPTION
Chair			
A	2	1-1/2" x 7-1/4" x 35" cedar	Back legs
B	1	1-1/2" x 5-1/2" x 22-1/4" cedar	Back top
C	2	1-1/2" x 3-1/2" x 25-1/4" cedar	Front legs
D	2	1-1/2" x 3-1/2" x 22-1/4" cedar	Back bottom and front seat support
E	2	3/4" x 3-1/2" x 23-1/2" cedar	Arms
F	2	3/4" x 3-1/2" x 14" cedar	Side seat supports
G	6	3/4" x 2-3/4" x 25-1/4" cedar	Seat slats
H	2	3/4" x 2" x 14" cedar	Side stretchers
J	9	3/4" x 1-1/2" x 13-1/2" cedar	Back slats
Love Seat			
A	2	1-1/2" x 7-1/4" x 34" cedar	Back legs
B	1	1-1/2" x 5-1/2" x 43-5/8" cedar	Back top
C	2	1-1/2" x 3-1/2" x 25-1/4" cedar	Front legs
D	2	1-1/2" x 3-1/2" x 43-5/8" cedar	Back bottom and front seat support
E	2	3/4" x 3-1/2" x 23-1/2" cedar	Arms
F	2	3/4" x 3-1/2" x 14" cedar	Side seat supports
G	6	3/4" x 2-3/4" x 46-5/8" cedar	Seat slats
H	2	3/4" x 2" x 14" cedar	Side stretchers
J	18	3/4" x 1-1/2" x 13-1/2" cedar	Back slats
K	1	1-1/2" x 3-1/2" x 16-1/4" cedar	Center seat support
Table			
A	4	1-1/2" x 2-1/2" x 19-1/4" cedar	Legs
B	4	3/4" x 4-1/2" x 13" cedar	Aprons
C	6	3/4" x 2-7/8" x 16-3/4" cedar	Top slats
D	2	3/4" x 2" x 13" cedar	Side stretchers

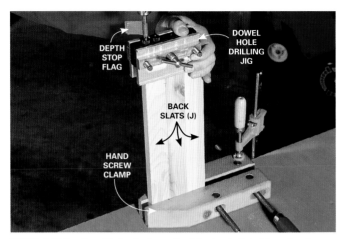

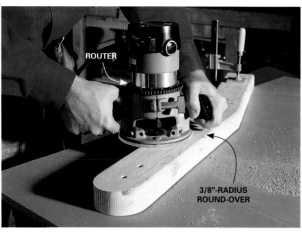

3 Drill the dowel holes in the ends of the back slats. Clamping the slats side by side like this gives the dowel-drilling jig more surface area to clamp onto.

4 Rout the edges of all the pieces (except the end cuts). Clamp the pieces to your work table, or use a router pad to hold the pieces as you rout them.

Materials list

ITEM	QTY.
Chair	
2x8 x 8' cedar	1 pc.
2x4 x 8' cedar	2 pcs.
1x4 x 8' cedar	4 pcs.
3/8"-dia. x 2" dowel pins	16
5/16"-dia. x 1-1/2" dowel pins	36
3" galvanized deck screws	12
1-5/8" galvanized deck screws	21
Love Seat	
2x8 x 8' cedar	1 pc.
2x6 x 8' cedar	1 pc.
2x4 x 8' cedar	2 pcs.
1x4 x 8' cedar	6 pcs.
3/8" dia. x 2" dowel pins	16
5/16" dia. x 1-1/2" dowel pins	72
3" galvanized deck screws	15
1-5/8" galvanized deck screws	28
Table	
2x4 x 8' cedar	1 pc.
1x6 x 8' cedar	1 pc.
1x4 x 8' cedar	2 pcs.
3/8" dia. x 2" dowel pins	16
3" galvanized deck screws	8
1-5/8" galvanized deck screws	12
Glue and finish for all three	
Weatherproof or waterproof glue	16 ozs.
Exterior deck stain	1 qt.
Mineral spirits to thin stain	2 qts.

1/4-in.-thick plywood, make full-size templates of the shapes for the back legs (A), chair back top (B), arms (E), and side seat supports (F). Start by cutting your template stock to the rectangular sizes shown in the patterns in Figure A. Draw a 1 x 1-in. grid on your template pieces, then transfer and enlarge the shapes from our drawings to your templates (Photo 1). Mark the screw locations too. Cut out the template shapes and sand the sawn edges smooth.

Cutting the parts

Cut all the pieces A through J to the dimensions given in the Cutting List. Trace the shapes from your completed templates onto the back legs, chair back top, and side seat supports (A, B and F). Cut out the shapes using a jigsaw or band saw, then sand the sawn edges smooth (Photo 2). You'll shape the arms after you assemble the chair by cutting and fitting the notches at the rear of the arms around the back legs.

Drilling screw and dowel holes

Lay out and drill the screw plug holes and screw clearance holes in the legs (A and C). Lay out and drill the dowel holes on the edges of the back top and back bottom (B and D), and in the ends of the side seat supports, side stretchers and back slats (F, H and J); see Photo 3.

Laying out the back slat dowel holes in the back top (B) and back bottom (D) can be a little tricky, so be careful. Don't measure from one mark to the next. Instead, add the dowel hole spread distances together, and measure and mark from one end with your tape measure. When you're done marking, double-check everything. Remember, you'll be using 5/16-in.-dia. dowels for these holes. To correctly mark these back-slat dowel hole locations, assume a spread of 3/4 in. between the dowel hole centers. The first hole center for the first slat is 1-1/4 in. from the end of B and D. The next hole center is another 3/4 in. from the first. The first hole center for the second slat is an additional 1-5/8 in. plus 3/4 in. for the next hole. For the first hole center for the third slat, measure an additional 1-5/8 in., then another 3/4 in. Continue this method until the last slat.

Routing and sanding

Now's the time to round some sharp edges and do some sanding before assembly. Mount a 3/8-in.-radius round-over bit in a router to rout the edges on the pieces (Photo 4). See Figure A for which edges to round. Leave the router set up this way to do the edges of the arms after the shapes are cut.

Using a belt sander first, then an orbital sander, finish-sand all the pieces. You'll still have a bit more to do later after the chair's assembled.

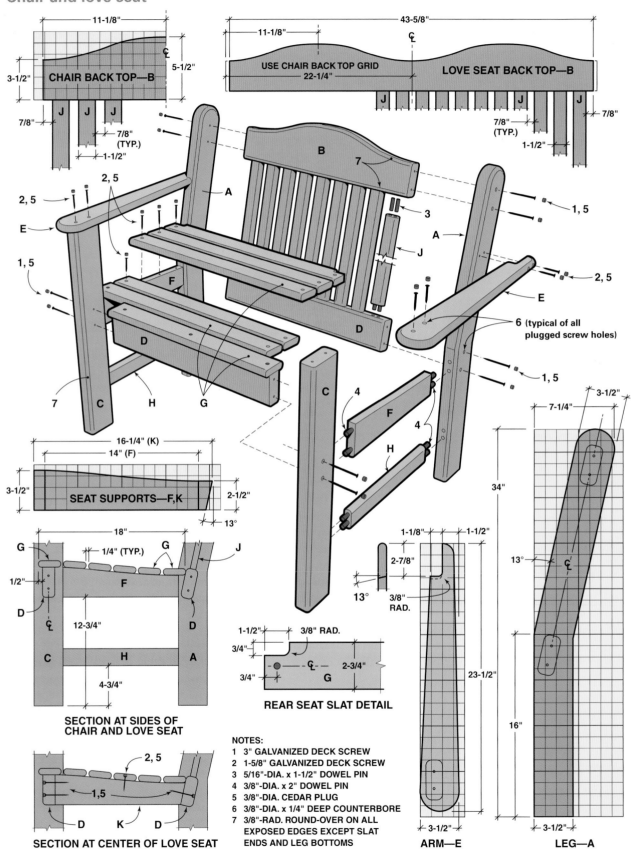

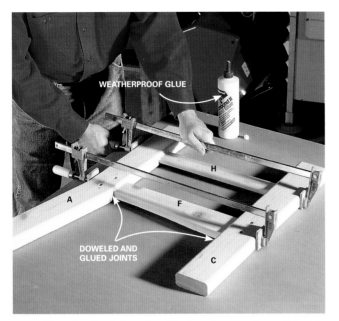

5 Glue, dowel and clamp the side pieces together. Be careful not to apply too much glue and create a mess.

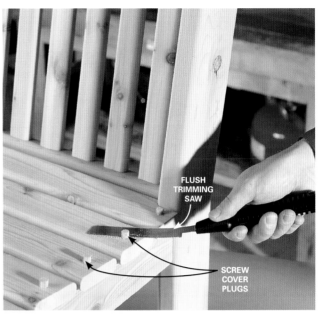

6 Use a flush-trimming saw or sharp chisel to trim off the heads of the screw cover plugs. Finish-sand them with a sanding block, then an orbital sander.

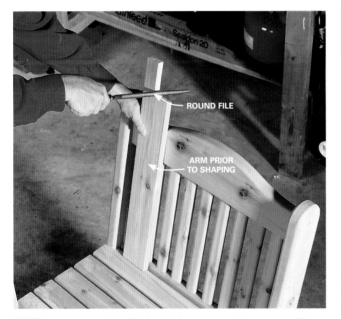

7 Using the partially finished chair as a convenient support, file the angled radiused corner of the arm notch so it fits around the back leg.

8 Align and clamp the arms to the front legs. Insert the screws that go into the back legs, remove the clamps and then screw the arms to the front legs.

Assemble the sides and back

Glue, dowel and clamp the side assemblies (A, C, F and H) together (Photo 5). Use a thin dowel or stick to spread the glue in the dowel holes. We found it was better to gently hammer the dowels in the ends of pieces F and H first. Putting dowels in the legs first may cause some of the ends of these pieces to split when all the pieces are assembled.

Glue, dowel and clamp the back pieces together (B, D and J). Start by inserting two dowels in one end of every back slat (J). Glue and clamp the back slats to the back top (B), one at a time. Insert the dowels in the other ends of the back slats. Then, with the help of a friend, align and attach the back bottom (D). Start at one end and work to the other end.

Align, glue and screw the sides to the assembled back and the front seat support (D). Once again, an extra set of hands is helpful here.

Figure B
Table

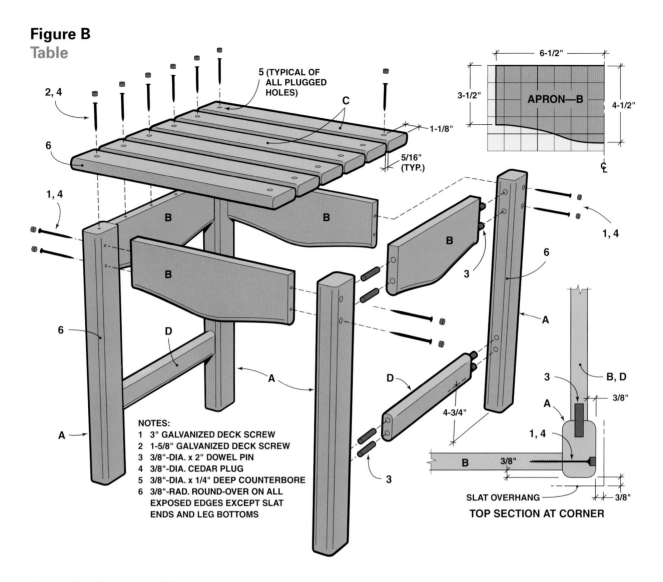

5 (TYPICAL OF ALL PLUGGED HOLES)

C

1-1/8"

5/16" (TYP.)

2, 4

6

1, 4

6

B

B

B

B

B

D

A

A

6

A

D

3

3

6-1/2"

3-1/2"

APRON—B

4-1/2"

Ȼ

1, 4

6

A

3

4-3/4"

3

B, D

3/8"

A

1, 4

B

3/8"

SLAT OVERHANG

3/8"

TOP SECTION AT CORNER

NOTES:
1 3" GALVANIZED DECK SCREW
2 1-5/8" GALVANIZED DECK SCREW
3 3/8"-DIA. x 2" DOWEL PIN
4 3/8"-DIA. CEDAR PLUG
5 3/8"-DIA. x 1/4" DEEP COUNTERBORE
6 3/8"-RAD. ROUND-OVER ON ALL
   EXPOSED EDGES EXCEPT SLAT
   ENDS AND LEG BOTTOMS

Attach the seat slats

Trim the length of the front seat slat (G) so it fits between the front legs. Cut the notched ends of the back seat slat as shown in Figure A and see that it fits between the back legs. Lay out and drill the screw plug and clearance holes (for the wood plugs) in the seat slats, then glue and screw the front and back seat slats in place. Attach the rest of the seat slats so the gaps between them are equal.

To make wood plugs to cover the recessed screws, use a 3/8-in.-dia. plug cutter. Glue and insert the plugs in the holes to cover the screws. Drill a shallow 3/4-in.-dia. hole in a piece of scrap wood. Fill the hole with glue and use it as a reservoir to dip the plugs in and apply the glue. When the glue is dry, trim off the tops of the plugs (Photo 6).

Attach the arms

Trace the back leg notches from your arm template to the arm pieces (E). Then cut out the notches using a jigsaw or band saw (see Figure A for the dimension and angle details). Make the final fit of the angled inside radiused corners using a round file (Photo 7). When that's done, trace and cut out the shapes of the arms and rout the rounded-over edges. Predrill the plug and screw holes, then finish-sand and attach the arms (Photo 8) with galvanized deck screws.

Apply the finish

You can protect your furniture with exterior deck stain as we described on p. 65. A clear exterior finish is another option, but it will slow down the aging process. It depends on the look you want. However, be sure you choose some type of waterproof finish to keep the pieces from drying out and splitting.

Adirondack chair & love seat

This chair and love seat combo is just perfect for outdoor lounging. The seat has a nice curved recess to conform to your body, and wide arms to hold your favorite snack and drink. And because the seat doesn't slope steeply downward like on a traditional Adirondack chair, even your grandfather will be able to get himself up without a boost.

You won't need an arsenal of power tools to build this furniture. In fact, you'll only need a circular saw, a drill and simple hand tools. We've designed this project for simplicity as well: With a bit of patience, even a novice can do a great job.

The wood is pressure-treated pine, chosen for its low cost, high strength and longevity. And don't worry about the drab green look of treated wood. You can brush on an exterior oil or latex stain and give it a beautiful warm glow that makes it look more like mahogany or teak than treated pine.

WHAT IT TAKES

TIME: 1 weekend
SKILL LEVEL: Beginner to intermediate

1 Clamp the two front legs together, measure for the 3/4-in. deep notch and make repeated cuts with your circular saw set to 3/4-in. depth of cut. Chisel the pieces between the cuts and then file smooth.

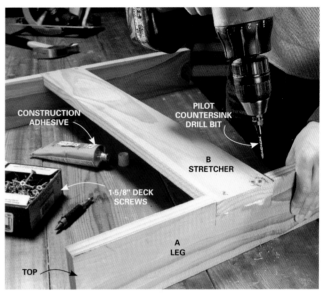

2 Spread a light bead of construction adhesive into each notch and align the front stretcher (B) with the edge of the legs. Drill and screw the stretcher to the legs.

3 Mark the angle on the back side of each arm and cut the arms (C) and arm supports (D) with your circular saw.

4 Align the arm supports with the top and front edges of the legs, then drill and screw each front leg to the arm support with two 1-5/8-in. deck screws.

Select straight, knot-free, pressure-treated pine

Most outdoor wood furniture is made from cedar or expensive teak, but regular treated boards from your home center or lumberyard are perfect for this project. The trick is to select boards that are as straight and free of knots as you can find.

A few tight knots are OK, and if you spot a board that looks great except for a huge loose knot, just cut it out and use the knot-free sections. It's a good idea to buy a couple of extra boards, just in case you end up cutting out more sections than you'd planned. Also avoid boards that are still wet from the treatment process (they'll feel cool and damp) because they might warp or crack as they dry.

Don't assume that the treated boards are dimensionally consistent. When we got our lumber, the boards varied by as much as 3/16 in. in width. These variations can screw up the assembly process, especially for the back slats, which require spacers to get an exact back width. Once you get the boards home and begin to cut the pieces, use a table saw or the rip guide on your circular saw

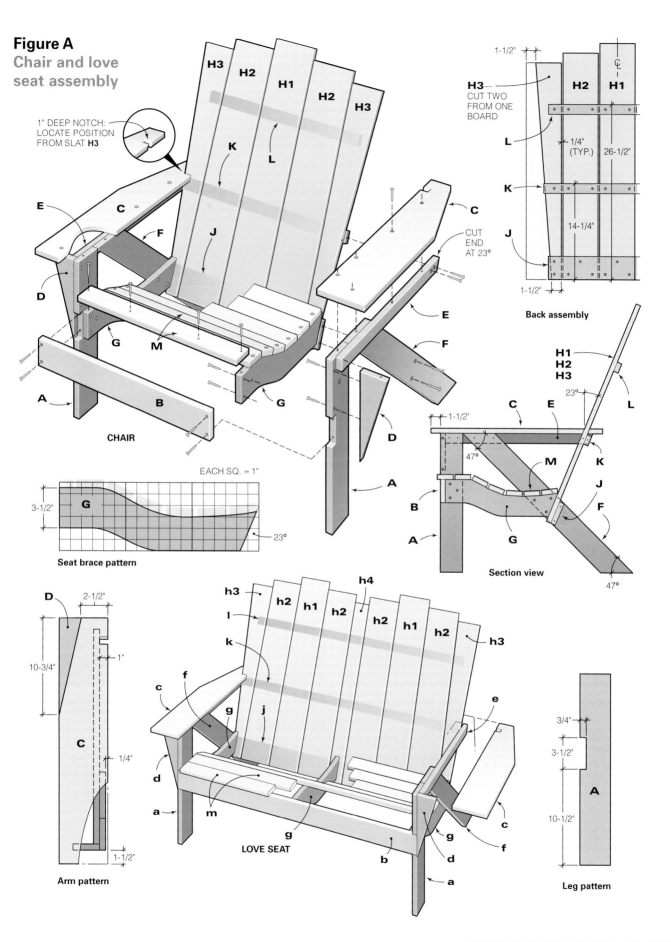

Figure A
Chair and love seat assembly

1" DEEP NOTCH:
LOCATE POSITION
FROM SLAT **H3**

H3

H2

H1

H2

H3

K

L

E

C

F

D

G

M

A

B

CHAIR

C

CUT
END
AT 23°

E

F

G

D

A

1-1/2"

H3
CUT TWO
FROM ONE
BOARD

H2   **H1**

L

1/4"
(TYP.)   26-1/2"

K

14-1/4"

J

1-1/2"

Back assembly

H1
H2
H3

23°

C   **E**

L

1-1/2"

47°

M

K

B

J

A

G

F

47°

Section view

EACH SQ. = 1"

3-1/2"

G

23°

Seat brace pattern

D

2-1/2"

10-3/4"

1"

C

1/4"

1-1/2"

Arm pattern

h3

h4

h2 **h1** **h2**

h2 **h1** **h2**

l

k

h3

f

c

g

j

e

d

a

m

g

g

c

f

d

b

a

LOVE SEAT

3/4"

3-1/2"

A

10-1/2"

Leg pattern

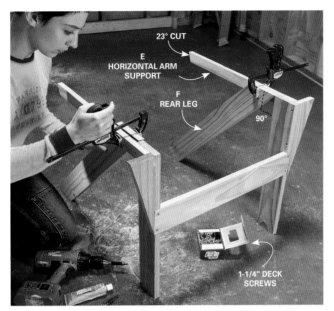

5 Fasten the horizontal arm supports (E) at 90 degrees to the front legs. Then glue, drill and screw the rear legs to the arm supports, making sure the arm supports are parallel to the floor.

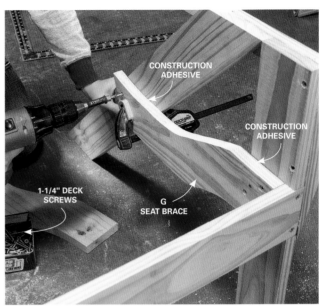

6 Cut the seat supports (G) from 1x6 boards. Align the square front edge of the seat brace with the back of the front stretcher (B) and glue and screw them to the front and back legs.

7 Mark a diagonal line on H3, then clamp the board to your sawhorses and cut along the line to make a pair of outer back slats.

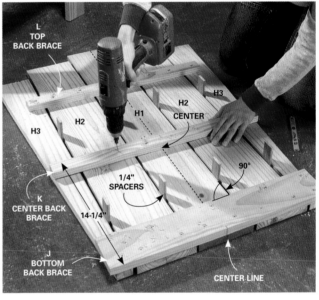

8 Set the back slats on a flat surface with 1/4-in.-wide spacers. Center the back braces on the slats. Glue, drill and screw them with 1-1/4-in. deck screws.

to trim them to the exact widths in the Cutting List. Or just let them dry out for a few weeks before assembly.

Assemble the main frame

Cut the notches in the front legs to accept the front stringer as shown in Photo 1. As you chisel out the waste wood in the notch, shave the bottom carefully and fine-tune it with a rasp to keep the notch from getting too deep.

As you assemble the basic frame (Photos 2 – 6), make sure your work surface is flat so each piece aligns with the adjoining pieces at the correct angle. Be sure to use a dab of construction adhesive in every joint and predrill a pilot and countersink hole for each screw. You

can buy a bit at your local hardware store that drills a pilot and countersink in one operation for the No. 6 screws.

Spacers make the back assembly a snap

To achieve the gentle taper of the back assembly, you'll need to taper the outer seat slat and cut it as shown in Photo 7.

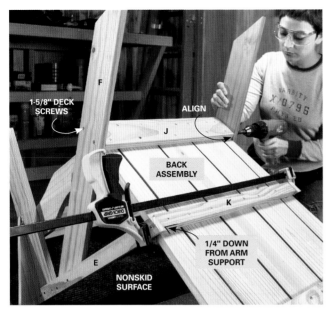

9 Align the bottom of the back assembly with the seat braces and the tops of the rear legs. Screw the legs to the back brace and screw the horizontal arm supports to the center back brace.

10 Space the seat slats (M), evenly starting at the back. Drill one pilot hole on each end of the slats and screw them to the seat brace. Screw the front seat slat to the seat brace as well as the front stretcher (B).

11 Set the arm flush with the edge of the arm support (E), overhanging the front leg 1-1/2 in. Mark the arm where it meets the back slat.

12 Notch the arm with a handsaw and fasten it to the horizontal support, the top edge of the back legs and to the front leg and arm support with 1-5/8-in. screws and glue.

First, place a mark 1-1/2 in. from the edge on opposite ends as shown. Connect the marks with a line and then saw right down the middle of the line with your circular saw. Sand or plane the cut edge to smooth away any saw marks.

Before you assemble the back of the chair or love seat, cut 1/4-in. thick spacers from scrap wood. The spacers (Photo 8) will ensure that the back assembly is the right width. Lay each slat on the floor and make sure the best-looking side of each board is facing down. As you screw the three back braces to the back slats, use a framing square to make sure they're perpendicular. You'll find it easier to get the proper alignment if you match the center point of each brace with the center line drawn down the middle back slat. Drill pilot holes and drive 1-1/4 in. deck screws through the braces into the slats as shown in Figure A and Photo 8.

Once you've assembled the back, it's time to fasten it to the chair frame. Flip the frame assembly upside down and insert the back assembly into it (Photo 9). This can be a bit challenging, so make it easier by laying two nonskid rugs or mats on the floor under the chair frame

Add a personal touch to your outdoor furniture

You can build our step-back version of the chair and love seat or experiment with other shapes to suit your sense of style. Feel free to try the gable or round back shown below or draw a different shape on paper, tape it to the chair and step back to see how you like it.

STEP BACK   **GABLE BACK**   **ROUND BACK**

PIVOT NAIL

Create a round back by measuring down 15 in. from the top and drawing a 14-in. radius with a homemade compass.

Cutting list for chair

KEY	QTY.	SIZE & DESCRIPTION
A	2	3/4" x 3-1/2" x 21" front legs
B	1	3/4" x 3-1/2" x 23" front stretcher
C	2	3/4" x 5-1/2" x 27" arms
D	2	3/4" x 3" x 10-3/4" triangular arm supports
E	2	3/4" x 1-1/2" x 23-1/4" horizontal arm supports
F	2	3/4" x 3-1/2" x 34-1/2" rear legs
G	2	3/4" x 5-1/2" x 17-3/4" seat braces
H1	1	3/4" x 5-1/2" x 35-3/4" center back slat
H2	2	3/4" x 5-1/2" x 34-1/4" inner back slats
H3	1	3/4" x 5-1/2" x 32-3/4" outer back slats (taper cut into two pieces)
J	1	3/4" x 3-1/2" x 21-1/2" bottom back brace
K	1	3/4" x 1-1/2" x 23" center back brace
L	1	3/4" x 1-1/2" x 21-1/2" top back brace
M	7	3/4" x 2-1/2" x 21-1/2" seat slats

Cutting list for love seat

KEY	QTY.	SIZE & DESCRIPTION
a	2	3/4" x 3-1/2" x 21" front legs
b	1	3/4" x 3-1/2" x 43" front stretcher
c	2	3/4" x 5-1/2" x 27" arms
d	2	3/4" x 3" x 10-3/4" triangular arm supports
e	2	3/4" x 1-1/2" x 23-1/4" horizontal arm supports
f	2	3/4" x 3-1/2" x 34-1/2" rear legs
g	3	3/4" x 5-1/2" x 17-3/4" seat braces
h1	2	3/4" x 5-1/2" x 35-3/4" back slats
h2	4	3/4" x 5-1/2" x 34-1/4" back slats
h3	1	3/4" x 5-1/2" x 32-3/4" outer back slat (taper cut into two pieces)
h4	1	3/4" x 2-1/2" x 32-3/4" center back slat (trim to fit)
j	1	3/4" x 3-1/2" x 41-1/2" bottom back brace
k	1	3/4" x 1-1/2" x 43" center back brace
l	1	3/4" x 1-1/2" x 41-1/2" top back brace
m	7	3/4" x 2-1/2" x 41-1/2" seat slats

and the top of the back assembly. These will help keep everything in place. As you align these assemblies, it's critical to get the back of the seat braces flush with the outer back slats (H3) and then screw through the rear legs into the bottom back brace (J) as shown in Photo 9 and Figure A. Next, glue and screw the horizontal arm supports (E) into the center back brace (K) and then into the side of the outer back slat as well.

With the completion of this phase, you'll start to see a chair emerging. Flip the chair onto its legs and cut and predrill the seat slats. Glue and screw

them to the seat braces with 1-5/8-in. deck screws (Photo 10). Don't overdrive the screws—the heads should be just flush with the seat slats. The last step of the assembly is to fasten the arms to the arm supports and the legs as shown in Photos 11 and 12. The notches you cut near the back of the arms hold the back assembly firmly in place and reduce the stress on the screws at other joints. These compound notches slice through the arm at an angle. Cut the depth carefully with a handsaw and then chisel out the notch. Brush on an exterior stain

Once the chair is assembled, ease

all the edges with 100-grit sandpaper, paying particular attention to the seat and arms. If the wood feels damp or cold to the touch, you may need to let the chair dry in a shaded area for a few days before you sand or stain it.

We used an oil-based cedar natural tone stain that lets the grain show through. Several options are available, including custom semi-transparent stains that a paint supplier can mix for you. A quart will easily do a pair of chairs or a chair and love seat. This finish will last at least several years and can be cleaned and recoated as it shows signs of wear.

Adirondack chair: version 2

WHAT IT TAKES

TIME: 1 weekend
SKILL LEVEL: Beginner to intermediate

P lop down in one of these solid wood chairs and you'll appreciate the comfort of this traditional design. You don't have to be an expert to build it either. All the parts can be cut with a circular saw and jigsaw, then assembled with a drill with a Phillips-tip bit, a few clamps and glue. Even if you're a novice, you'll be able to follow our plan drawing and clear step-by-step photos. And the Materials List and Cutting List will help you spend less time head-scratching and more time building.

We made our chair from yellow poplar. Poplar is lightweight,

strong, inexpensive and easy to work with, plus it takes paint beautifully. If you have trouble finding it, almost any other wood will do: Alder, aspen, maple and white oak are excellent hardwood choices, and cedar, cypress, fir and pine are good softwood choices. Keep in mind that hardwood will be more durable, but softwood is certainly strong enough for this project.

Traditional Adirondack chairs are painted, but you can choose a clear outdoor deck finish if you prefer. If you do opt for paint, check out the painting tips on p. 81 to help achieve a tough, long-lasting and good-looking painted finish.

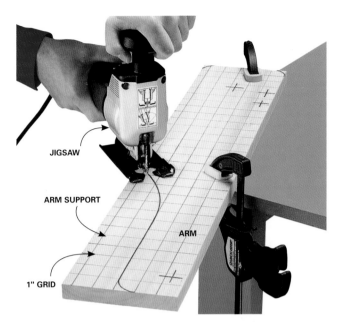

1 Draw full-size grids onto the arm and back leg pieces and follow the curves with a jigsaw.

JIGSAW

ARM SUPPORT

ARM

1" GRID

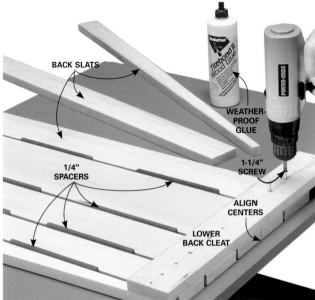

2 Slip 1/4-in. spacers between the back slats as you screw the horizontal back supports (G, L and N) to the slats. Predrill and countersink each hole and apply weatherproof glue to each joint.

BACK SLATS

WEATHER-PROOF GLUE

1/4" SPACERS

1-1/4" SCREW

ALIGN CENTERS

LOWER BACK CLEAT

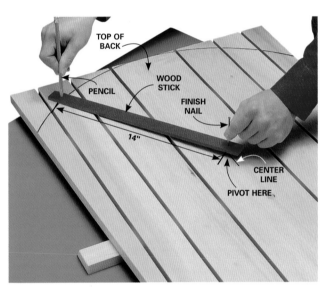

3 Make a compass from a scrap of wood by drilling a hole near each end. Put a nail in one end and use a pencil in the other hole to draw the 14-in. radius to form the curved top.

TOP OF BACK

PENCIL

WOOD STICK

FINISH NAIL

14"

CENTER LINE

PIVOT HERE

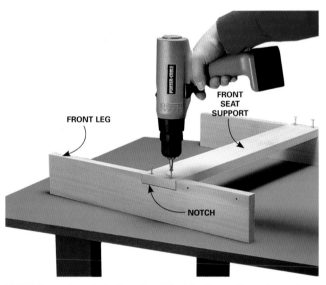

4 Cut and notch the front legs (E) with a jigsaw. Then glue and screw the front seat support into the notches.

FRONT LEG

FRONT SEAT SUPPORT

NOTCH

Transfer the grid patterns

Enlarge the grids directly onto the board, or make a full-size pattern and transfer the shape to the board.

Once the shape is drawn, follow the lines with a jigsaw (Photo 1). Write "pattern" on the first leg and arm pieces and use them to make the others. If you're making more than one chair, now's the time to trace all the arm and leg pieces for each chair. The left arms and legs are mirror images of the right. Also, trim the small cutout piece of each arm (C) to make the arm support (K) for each side.

Cut the tapered back pieces

The two tapered back pieces are tricky to cut, and the safest way to do it is to cut them from a wider board. Draw the tapers shown in Figure A onto a 1x6 cut to length. Nail each end of the board to the tops of a sawhorse, placing the nails where they'll be out of the saw's path. Use a No. 4 finish nail on each end and hammer it in flush with the surface. Set the depth of your circular saw 1/8 in. deeper than the thickness of the board, and cut the taper from the wide end to the narrow end. Next, draw a straight line on the remaining part to define the second piece and cut it. Note: Before you begin assembly,

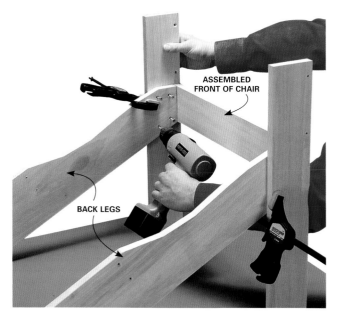

5 Clamp the back legs (B) to the front assembly to accurately position them. Work on a flat workbench surface so the chair won't wobble. Apply glue, drill pilot holes and drive 1-1/4-in. deck screws.

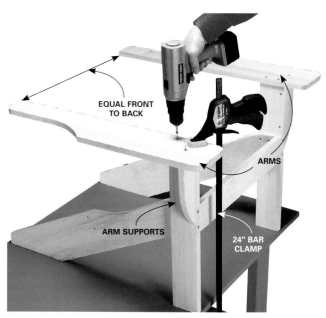

6 Glue and screw on the arm supports (K). Then glue and screw the arms to the front legs and arm supports. Use clamps to position the arms so they overhang the insides of the front legs by 1/4 in.

sand all the pieces and ease the edges with 100-grit sandpaper, followed by 150-grit.

Assemble the back first

Lay the back pieces face down on your workbench (Photo 2). Line up the bottoms and insert 1/4-in. spacers between the slats. Cut your 1/4-in. spacers from scrap boards or scrap 1/4-in. plywood. Screw each of the horizontal back supports G, L and N to the slats with 1-1/4- in. exterior deck screws. Predrill and

Materials list

ITEM	QTY.
1x6 x 10' poplar	1 piece
1x6 x 8' poplar	1 piece
1x6 x 12' poplar	1 piece
1x4 x 12' poplar	1 piece
1-5/8" galvanized deck screws	24
1-1/4" galvanized deck screws	68
Exterior oil primer	1 qt.*
White exterior gloss enamel	1 qt.*

*Enough paint to finish two chairs

Cutting list

KEY	PCS.	SIZE & DESCRIPTION
A	1	3/4" x 5-1/2" x 35" poplar (center back slat)
B	2	3/4" x 5-1/2" x 33" poplar (back legs)
C	2	3/4" x 5-1/2" x 29" poplar (arms)
D	1	3/4" x 3-1/2" x 23" poplar (front seat support)
E	2	3/4" x 3-1/2" x 21" poplar (front legs)
F	2	3/4" x 3-1/4" x 35" poplar (back slats)
G	1	3/4" x 3" x 20" poplar (lower back cleat)
H	4	3/4" x 2-1/2" x 35" poplar (back slats)
J	6	3/4" x 2-1/2" x 21-1/2" poplar (seat slats)
K	2	3/4" x 2-1/2" x 9" poplar (arm supports)‡
L	1	3/4" x 2" x 25-1/2" poplar (center back support)
M	1	3/4" x 2" x 21-1/2" poplar (back leg support)
N	1	3/4" x 2" x 21" poplar (upper back support)

‡Cut from pieces C

countersink each screw hole.

You'll need to cut a bevel on the top side of the center horizontal back support (L). A table saw works best, but you could use the same circular saw method you used earlier to cut the tapered side back slats (H). Just set the bevel on your circular saw to 33 degrees, nail the 1x6 board to the sawhorses, mark the width and make the cut.

With a framing square, check that the back slats and horizontal supports are positioned 90 degrees to each other as you glue and screw the assembly (Photo 2). Once the back is fastened, turn the back assembly over, mark the top radius and trim it with a jigsaw (Photo 3). Screw the chair frame together Using your jigsaw, cut the notches on parts E as shown in Figure A. Glue and screw the front seat support (D) to the front legs (Photo 4). Next set the front assembly vertically on your workbench and glue and screw the back legs B to the front legs (Photo 5). Again, drill pilot and countersink holes for each screw. Then glue and screw the arm supports to the outer sides

> **Work smart**
>
> When you're building more than one chair, set up an assembly line and cut the building time per chair by 40 percent.

Figure A
Adirondack chair, version 2

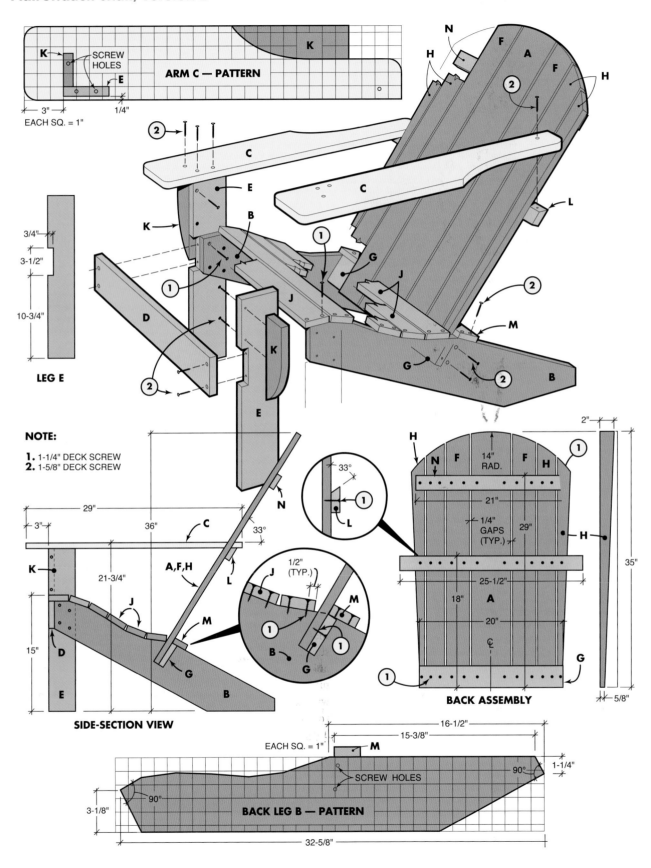

ARM C — PATTERN

SCREW HOLES

K

E

3"

1/4"

EACH SQ. = 1"

N

F

A

H

F

H

2

C

C

L

3/4"

3-1/2"

10-3/4"

LEG E

B

K

D

E

K

G

J

J

2

M

G

G

2

B

E

N

NOTE:

1. 1-1/4" DECK SCREW
2. 1-5/8" DECK SCREW

29"

3"

36"

C

33°

21-3/4"

A,F,H

K

L

J

N

1

33°

L

1

1/2" (TYP.)

J

M

1

1

B

G

G

H

N

F

14" RAD.

F

H

2"

1

21"

1/4" GAPS (TYP.)

29"

H

25-1/2"

18"

A

20"

35"

15"

D

E

J

M

G

B

SIDE-SECTION VIEW

1

BACK ASSEMBLY

G

5/8"

16-1/2"

15-3/8"

M

EACH SQ. = 1"

1-1/4"

90°

SCREW HOLES

90°

3-1/8"

BACK LEG B — PATTERN

32-5/8"

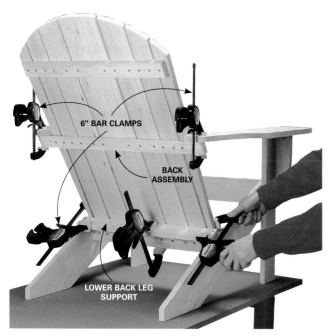

6" BAR CLAMPS

BACK
ASSEMBLY

LOWER BACK LEG
SUPPORT

7 Glue, clamp and screw the lower back leg support (M) to the back legs first. Then glue and clamp the back assembly, first to the back legs, then to the arm supports. Drill pilot and countersink holes for the screws.

1/4" GAPS

SEAT SLATS

8 Predrill all the pilot and countersink holes in the seat slats before you position them. Screw the seat slats (J) to the back legs with 1-1/4-in. deck screws (use 1-5/8-in. screws in softwood), spacing them 1/4 in. apart.

of the front legs (E).

Position the arms on the tops of the front legs and the arm supports (K). Make sure the arms hang 3 in. over the front leg and 1/4 in. over the inside edge of each leg. Before fastening the arms, make sure they're parallel (Photo 6).

Screw the back leg support (M) to each leg (see Figure A) and then set the back assembly into the frame and clamp it in place (Photo 7). Make sure the back of each arm projects 3/4 in. past the center back support (L). Glue and predrill each joint, screw the assembly together and then remove the clamps.

To finish the assembly, predrill and countersink holes in the ends of the seat slats. Position them approximately 1/4 in. apart and screw them to the back legs as shown. Use a power screwdriver where possible, and a hand screwdriver in tight places.

Painting tips

You can use either a water-based or oil-based exterior primer and enamel topcoat.

Start applying the primer with the chair upside down. Use a 1-in.-wide sash brush for coating the edges of the seat slats, and then use a 3-in.-wide roller to apply primer to the flat surfaces and a 2-in. brush to smooth out the primer. Prime the back, then turn the chair over and prime the other surfaces in the same manner.

Let the primer dry overnight, then use a paint scraper to remove any runs and 120-grit sandpaper to lightly sand the entire surface. Apply the topcoat in the same order you applied the primer, then let the paint dry for at least three days before use.

6 YARD PROJECTS

Simple retaining wall

WHAT IT TAKES

TIME: 1 weekend
SKILL LEVEL: Beginner

his 32-in.-high, 32-ft.-long wall was built in one fairly laid-back day, by two fairly laid-back DIYers and a skid steer loader (Photo 7). They hired a skid steer loader operator and his machine. Having the loader meant there was very little shovel work.

The skeleton of the wall is a treated wood, 2x4 stud wall clad on both sides with 1/2-in. treated plywood. It's held in place with 2x4 "dead men" assemblies buried in the backfill. The dead men are 2x4 struts bolted to the wall studs and anchored to a perpendicular 2x4 sleeper (see Figure A). The weight of the soil on the dead men anchors the wall against the backfill pressure. It's important to locate the bottom of the wall below grade a few inches so the earth in front of the wall will anchor the base in place.

Get the right stuff

Ordinary treated wood will last a good long time depending on soil conditions, although wet sites with clay will shorten the wall's life somewhat. If you use ordinary treated wood from the home center, figure the wall will last at least 20 years. To build a wall that'll last forever, use foundation-grade treated wood, the material used for basements. It's usually Southern yellow pine, a very strong softwood that accepts treatment better than most, and contains a higher concentration of preservatives. You may find it at lumberyards where

contractors shop. Or you can special-order it from any home center or lumberyard, although you'll pay a premium.

Choose nails rated for treated wood: 16d for the framing and 8d for the sheathing. Use 3-in. construction screws for standoffs and dead men connections—again, ones that are rated for treated wood. You'll also need a box each of 2- and 3-in. deck screws for the trim boards. See the Materials List on p. 86.

Prepping the site

This site had a gentle slope to retain, not a huge hill. This 32-in.-high wall is designed to hold back a gentle slope and is good for walls up to 40 in. For walls 40 to 48 in. place the studs on 12-in. centers and keep the rest of the wall the same. Don't build the wall more than 48 in. high—a taller wall requires special engineering.

Do the digging with a shovel if you wish. The trick is to dig halfway into the hill and throw the soil on top of the hill. That way you'll have enough fill left for behind the wall. The downside is that if you hand-dig, you'll also need to dig channels for the 2x4 struts and sleepers (see Photo 5).

It's much easier to hire a skid steer loader and an operator to dig into the hill and then cut down a foot or so behind the wall to create a shelf for resting the dead men. The operator can also scoop out the 12-in.-wide by 10-in.-deep trench for the gravel footing, and deliver and dump a 6-in. layer of gravel into the footing. Then you'll only need to do a bit of raking to level off the trench. A yard of gravel will take care of 50 linear feet of wall. If you have extra gravel, use it for backfill against the back of the wall for drainage. Have the skid steer and operator return to fill against the back side of the wall and do some final grading.

Get the footings ready

Fill the trench with gravel. Any type will do, but pea gravel is the easiest to work with. Roughly rake it level, then tip one of the footing plates on edge and rest a level on top to grade the footing (Photo 1). Use the plate as a screed, as if you're leveling in concrete, and you'll get it really close, really fast. Try to get it within 1/4 in. or so of level. Offset any footing plate joints at least 2 ft. to either side of wall joints. To drive down the plate until it's level, stand on it as you pound it into the gravel with another board, occasionally checking it with a level. If you can't drive the board down to achieve level, scoop out shallow trenches on either side of the footing plate with your hand. Then there will be a place for gravel to flow as you drive down the plate.

Frame and set the walls

Frame the walls in your driveway or on the garage floor. The walls are very light, so you can carry them a long way if you need to. Build them in sections, whatever length you like, and screw the end studs together at the site. Leave off the sheathing for now. Snap a chalk line 1 in. in from the outside of the footing plate to align the walls (Photo 2). Place them, screw the joining studs together with four 3-in. construction screws and screw the wall plates to the footing plates in every other stud space with 3-in. construction screws.

Plumb, straighten and brace the walls from the front side and then add the tie plate. Make sure to seam the tie plate joints at least 4 ft. away from the wall joints. Sheathe and waterproof the walls

Set the plywood panels in place one at a time. Draw and cut 1-5/8-in. x 3-5/8-in.

Figure A
Wall anatomy

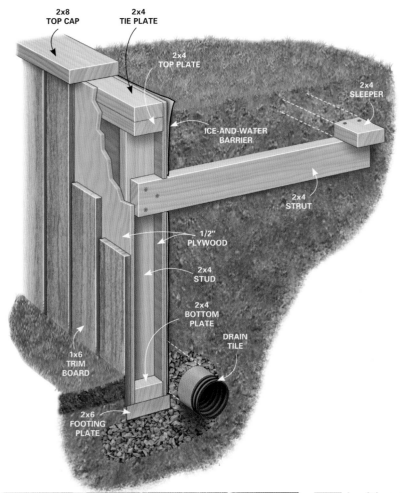

- 2x8 TOP CAP
- 2x4 TIE PLATE
- 2x4 TOP PLATE
- 2x4 SLEEPER
- ICE-AND-WATER BARRIER
- 2x4 STRUT
- 1/2" PLYWOOD
- 2x4 STUD
- 2x4 BOTTOM PLATE
- DRAIN TILE
- 1x6 TRIM BOARD
- 2x6 FOOTING PLATE

1 Level the gravel base. Lay the 2x6 footing plates on edge and use a 4-ft. level to level the gravel. Pack the gravel with the footing plate to drive it down until it's flat and level.

FOOTING PLATE

2 Frame and set the walls. Frame the walls and stand them on top of the footing plates. Snap a chalk line on the footing plate 1 in. from the edge and then screw the bottom plates to the footing plate even with the line.

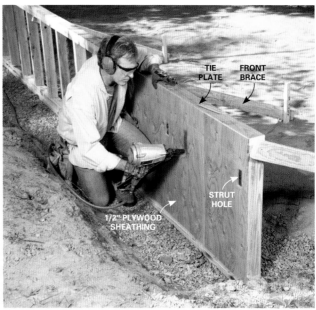

3 Brace and sheathe the wall. Plumb and brace the wall, then screw down the tie plate. Dry-fit the plywood to the back of the framing, mark the strut holes and cut out the holes. Then nail the plywood to the studs.

4 Waterproof the walls. Clad the back of the wall with ice-and-water barrier and cut out the strut holes with a utility knife.

5 Assemble the dead men. Poke the struts through the holes and screw them to each stud. Roughly prop up the struts and secure a continuous 2x4 sleeper to the end of each one with two 3-in. screws.

openings spaced 6 in. down from the underside of the top plate and directly next to every other stud. Nail each panel into place with 8d nails spaced every 8 in. before moving on to the next one. Cover the outside with ice-and-water barrier (Photo 4). The adhesive won't hold the barrier in place, so staple it as needed. Cut off the excess at the top and cut out the strut openings with a utility knife.

Add the struts and sleepers

Slip the struts through each hole. Prop them up so they're close to level, either by piling up dirt or supporting them on chunks of scrap wood. Screw each one to a stud with three 3-in. construction screws. (Predrill the holes to prevent splitting since it's so near the end.) Screw the sleeper to the other end of each strut with two more screws.

6 Add the trim. Nail vertically oriented plywood to the top and bottom plates and to the front of the wall. Make sure to seam plywood over studs. Screw a 2x8 top cap to the top plate, hanging it over the front of the wall 1-1/2 in. Fasten vertical 1x6s to the sheathing with 1-1/2-in. spaces between boards.

7 Time to backfill. Plumb and brace the wall from the back. Backfill, starting at the sleeper, to anchor the wall into place as you continue filling the space behind the wall.

Skin and finish the front

Before you can finish the front of the wall and backfill behind it, you'll have to remove the front braces. So prop up the dead men to keep the wall near plumb while you finish the front. Cut the plywood and nail it on, orienting it vertically to the front so the exposed grain will match the 1x6 boards applied over them. Add the 2x8 cap, keeping a 1-1/2-in. overhang at the front. Screw it to the tie plate with 3-in. deck screws. Screw the 1x6 treated boards to the sheathing with 2-in. deck screws. These boards are spaced every 1-1/2 in. using a scrap 2x4 as a spacer. Don't trust the spacer for more than a few boards at a time. Occasionally check a board with a level and make any necessary adjustments.

Backfill and finish

Plumb and brace the wall from the back by nailing braces to the top cap and stake them on the hill. Prop up every other strut and the sleepers with scraps of wood or the fill falling on the struts and sleepers will force the wall out of plumb. Backfill first against the front of the wall over the footing to lock the wall base into place, then fill behind it. Then fill over the sleeper, working your way toward the wall itself. The object is to lock in the sleeper before the fill pushes against the wall. Once the backfill is in place, it's a good idea to run a sprinkler over the fill for several hours to make it settle before you remove the braces.

If you like the look of your wall, you're good to go—no finish required. The treated wood will weather from green to gray in a year or two. Here, two coats of exterior stain was applied.

Materials list

This 32-ft.-long wall required the materials listed below. If you're building a shorter or longer wall, just figure a percentage of these quantities and you'll get close.

ITEM	QTY.
Roll of ice-and-water barrier	1
50' roll of 4" drain tile	1
Sheets of 1/2" plywood (sheathing)	8
2x6 x 16' (footing plates)	2
2x4 x 8' (studs and struts)	20
2x4 x 16' (sleeper and wall plates)	8
2x8 x 16' (top cap)	2
1x6 x 8' (trim boards)	20

Simple deck

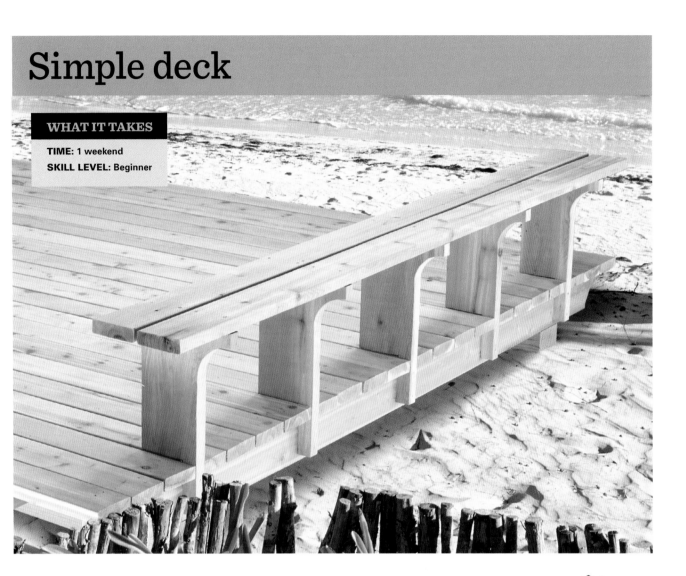

WHAT IT TAKES

TIME: 1 weekend
SKILL LEVEL: Beginner

Just follow these step-by-step photos

We can't promise you a beachfront view, but we know you'll enjoy relaxing on this simple deck wherever you choose to build it. Since it's at ground level and is freestanding, you don't have to fuss with challenging railings or footings. All you need are basic carpentry tools and a relatively flat area in your yard or garden. The foundation is nothing more than 4x6 treated timbers buried in the soil, with decorative treated joists and construction-grade cedar decking and a bench. Follow the instructions along with the photos for detailed measurements and building techniques.

Here's ALL the lumber you'll need, color-coded to our plans and photos.

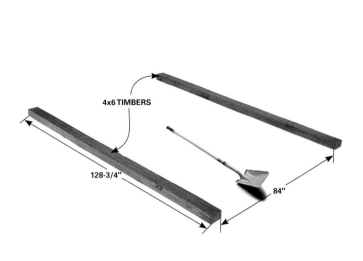

4x6 TIMBERS

128-3/4"

84"

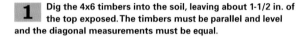

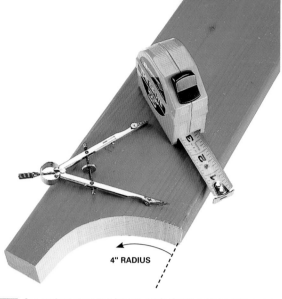

4" RADIUS

1 Dig the 4x6 timbers into the soil, leaving about 1-1/2 in. of the top exposed. The timbers must be parallel and level and the diagonal measurements must be equal.

2 Cut each treated 2x6 joist to 10 ft. Cut the decorative curve on each end, as shown, before installing them onto the 4x6 treated timbers.

Tool list

Shovel
Square
Tape measure
Level
Compass
Chalk line
Jigsaw
Hammer
Circular saw
Hearing and eye protection
Gloves

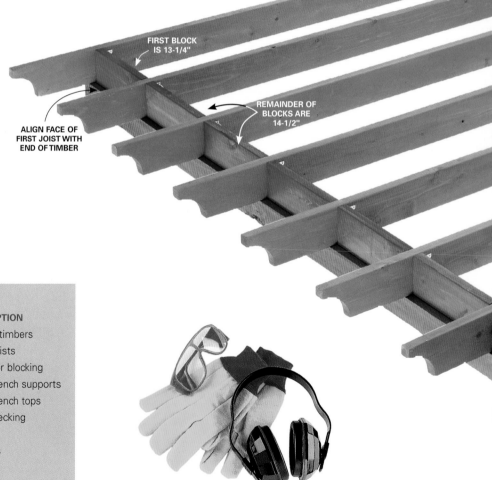

FIRST BLOCK IS 13-1/4"

REMAINDER OF BLOCKS ARE 14-1/2"

ALIGN FACE OF FIRST JOIST WITH END OF TIMBER

Materials list

QTY.	SIZE	DESCRIPTION
2	4x6 x 12'	treated timbers
9	2x6 x 10'	cedar joists
2	2x6 x 10'	cedar for blocking
1	2x12 x10'	cedar bench supports
2	2x6 x 10'	cedar bench tops
22	2x6 x 12'	cedar decking
32		metal corner brackets
3 lbs.		galv. joist hanger nails
2 lbs.		No. 8 galv. box nails
10 lbs.		16d galv. casing nails
1 lb.		3-in. galv. deck screws

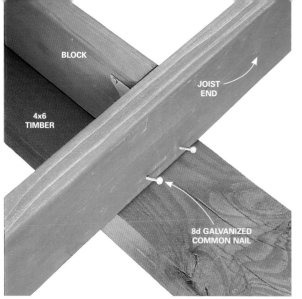

BLOCK

JOIST END

4x6 TIMBER

8d GALVANIZED COMMON NAIL

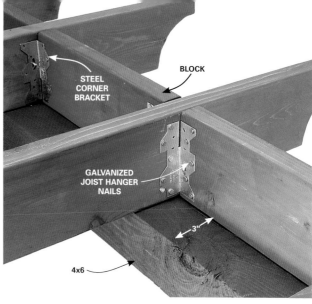

STEEL CORNER BRACKET

BLOCK

GALVANIZED JOIST HANGER NAILS

3"

4x6

3 Lay out the joist spacing so the joists are on 16-in. centers. Cut the blocks to fit between the joists. The first set of blocks (one on each side) will be 13-1/4 in., while the remainder will be 14-1/2 in. long. Toenail each joist to the timber as shown. Be sure the ends of all the joists align with each other as you toenail them in place.

4 Nail your steel corner brackets to the joists and each block between with 1-1/4-in. galvanized joist hanger nails. The blocks add stability and give the deck a finished look.

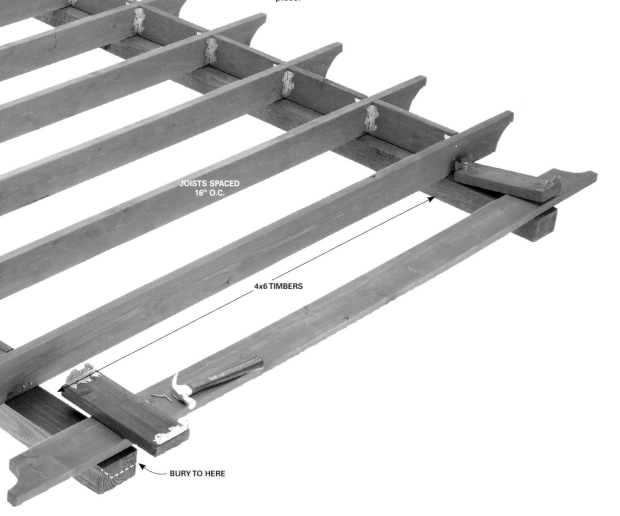

JOISTS SPACED 16" O.C.

4x6 TIMBERS

BURY TO HERE

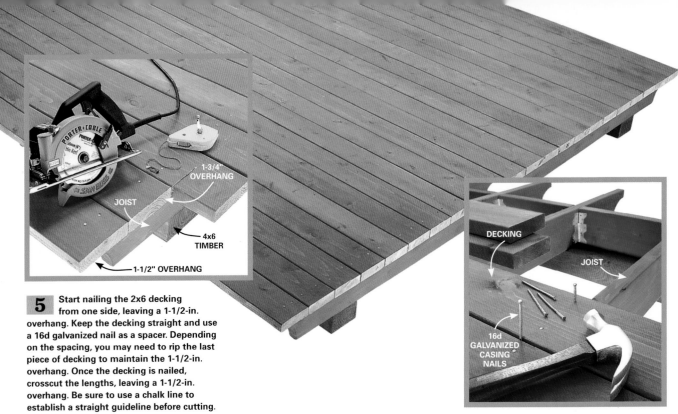

1-3/4" OVERHANG

JOIST

4x6 TIMBER

1-1/2" OVERHANG

DECKING

JOIST

16d GALVANIZED CASING NAILS

5 Start nailing the 2x6 decking from one side, leaving a 1-1/2-in. overhang. Keep the decking straight and use a 16d galvanized nail as a spacer. Depending on the spacing, you may need to rip the last piece of decking to maintain the 1-1/2-in. overhang. Once the decking is nailed, crosscut the lengths, leaving a 1-1/2-in. overhang. Be sure to use a chalk line to establish a straight guideline before cutting.

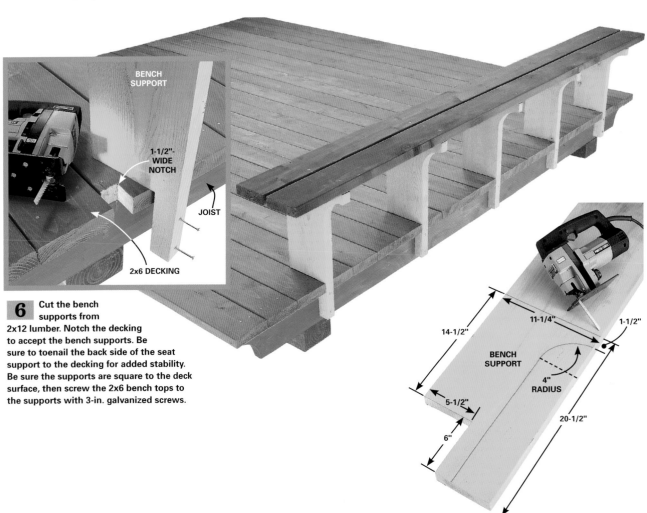

BENCH SUPPORT

1-1/2"-WIDE NOTCH

JOIST

2x6 DECKING

BENCH SUPPORT

14-1/2"

11-1/4"

1-1/2"

4" RADIUS

5-1/2"

6"

20-1/2"

6 Cut the bench supports from 2x12 lumber. Notch the decking to accept the bench supports. Be sure to toenail the back side of the seat support to the decking for added stability. Be sure the supports are square to the deck surface, then screw the 2x6 bench tops to the supports with 3-in. galvanized screws.

1-day patio pond

WHAT IT TAKES

TIME: 1 day, plus drying time
SKILL LEVEL: Beginner

If you can build a box, you can do it!

Getting started

Cut the two bottom boards (A and E; see Figure A, p. 95) to length. Cuts made at the lumber mill are usually rough, so trim the ends of all the boards before measuring.

Join all the components with both trim- head screws and construction adhesive. Adhesive works better than wood glue on rough-sawn lumber and is more forgiving on joints that aren't super tight. Apply a bead of adhesive and clamp the two bottom boards together. Scrape off the excess adhesive with a putty knife, and clean the rest with mineral spirits.

Install temporary cleats on the smooth side of the boards, which will be the inside of the container (Photo 1). Hold them in place with 1-1/4-in. screws. We used cabinet screws, but other types of screws would work just fine. Don't worry about

the screw holes left behind when you remove the cleats; the liquid rubber will fill them in.

Cut the boards to size

The width of 1x12s can vary slightly, so double-check the width of the bottom before you cut the ends and dividers (B and C) to length. The rough-sawn cedar we used was 7/8 in. thick. If you're working with material that's only 3/4 in. thick, you'll have to adjust the length of the sides.

All the trim parts are made from 1x6s ripped in half. Some home centers sell 1x3 boards, so you wouldn't have to bother with ripping at all.

Assemble the container

Mark guidelines for the dividers with a framing square 14 in. in from the ends of the bottom. Transfer that line to the inside of the sides (D). Face the smooth sides of the dividers toward the center compartment. That will ensure more even coverage of the liquid rubber in the compartment where it matters most.

Attach the ends and dividers to the bottom with adhesive and three 1-1/2-in. exterior-grade trim-head screws (Photo 2). Join the sides with adhesive and screws, three in each side of each end and divider. Space the screws about 10 in. apart along the bottom. The end caps hide the end grain and strengthen the corners. Secure them with four screws and adhesive. Cedar isn't as prone to splitting as harder woods, so predrill holes for screws only in areas where a knot is in your way.

Install four aluminum angle brackets (Photo 3). Cut them to size with a hacksaw or a jigsaw fitted with a bimetal blade. Drill two holes in each side, and secure them with adhesive and 3/4-in. screws.

Assemble the base with two 3-in. screws into each joint. It's easier to center the base when the container is upside down. Hold it in place by driving in four screws at an angle. Flip the whole thing over and secure the base to the container with 3-in. screws

A simple box with a rubber lining

We wanted a super-easy-to-build water feature, so we designed this wooden box that just about anyone can build with basic tools. What makes it work as a pond is a paint-on rubber lining. There are a few different brands of liquid rubber; check online. It's ultra-stretchy and UV-stable, and it can be used on lots of materials, including wood, metal and concrete. It's amazing stuff, though expensive.

You can use liquid rubber to fix leaky gutters and metal roofs, seal RVs and trailers, and for many other applications. Ranchers love it for sealing leaks in metal water tanks. And we love it because it can turn just about anything, even a simple wooden box, into a water feature.

driven down through the bottom of the container.

After removing the temporary cleats, drill four 1/2-in. drainage holes in the corners of the outside compartments and one in the middle. If you plan to install a water pump, drill a 1-1/2-in. hole for the cord with a hole saw. Figure out which side of the container has the best-looking wood grain and drill the hole on the opposite side about 3/8 in. down from the top edge.

Poor man's pocket hole

If you're a regular weekend woodworker, you really ought to get yourself a pocket hole jig. But if you don't have one, here's a quick and easy trick that works well on soft woods like cedar: Start by laying out the face frame, rough side down, and marking two guidelines at each joint. Then drill 1/8-in. holes through the end grain at an angle so the drill bit pops out about 3/4 in. to 7/8 in. down from the end of the board (Photo 4). At that length, a 1-1/2-in. trim-head screw will travel about 3/4 in. into the adjoining frame section. If you mess up and drill at a funky angle, you can always drill another hole a little bit over, and no one will be the wiser because it's on the underside of the face frame.

Build the face frame

Assemble the sides and the ends of the face frame with two 1-1/2-in. trim-head screws and adhesive (Photo 4). Keep downward pressure on both trim boards while driving in the first screw. A wood clamp on the seam works well as a third hand. Before installing the face frame dividers, measure diagonally from one corner to the other both ways to make sure the frame is square. If the frame is a little out of whack, adjust the frame until it's square, and clamp it to your workbench to hold it square.

Apply the liquid rubber and wood finish

Tape off the top edge of the container, the power cord hole and the drainage holes on the bottom. Brush the rubber

1 **Build the bottom.** Glue the bottom boards together with construction adhesive, and install three temporary cleats to hold them together until the project has been assembled.

2 **Install the dividers.** Fasten the dividers to the bottom, and then add the sides. Join all the parts with both adhesive and trim-head screws. Scrape any excess adhesive with a putty knife.

3 **Add corner brackets.** Cut aluminum angle stock to create corner brackets. Drill four holes in each bracket, and secure them with adhesive and screws.

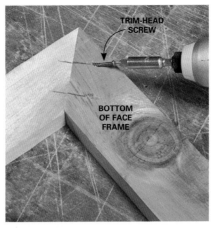

TRIM-HEAD SCREW

BOTTOM OF FACE FRAME

4 Build the face frame. Join the face-frame parts so that the new screws will be invisible. First, drill pilot holes through the end of one part (left photo). Then just hold the parts together and drive in screws (right photo).

5 Apply the liquid rubber. Glob a thick coat of the liquid rubber into all the seams, corners and defects in the wood. Apply one coat on the outside compartments and three on the middle.

6 Secure the face frame. Clamp the face frame into place and hold it down with adhesive and trim-head screws. Leave the screw heads flush with the surface to avoid pockets where water can pool and penetrate the wood.

on thick into the corners, seams, screw holes and defects in the wood (Photo 5). It takes three heavy coats to make a watertight seal and at least three hours between coats. Apply only one coat in the two outside compartments because they'll be filled with soil rather than water. Also apply just one coat on the very top edge of the container. Avoid blocking the drainage and cord holes with rubber by mopping the excess out with a cotton swab or rolled-up paper towel. The rubber needs to dry for a few days before it's ready for water.

Rough-sawn cedar isn't supposed to be smooth; hence the name. So resist the urge to sand, and embrace the imperfections. We applied a cedar-tinted wood finish, but any exterior stain or clear finish would work.

Finish up and add water

Once the finishes are dry, clamp the face to the container and fasten it with adhesive and 1-1/2-in. trim-head screws spaced every 10 in. or so (Photo 6). Set the screws flush with the surface of the wood to keep water from pooling.

A water pump isn't necessary but does help the water stay fresh. Some pumps have suction cups to hold them to the bottom, but the rubber-coated wood may not be smooth enough for them to stick. You can lay down a small chunk of Plexiglas at the bottom and stick the pump's suction cups to that. Floating water plants with exposed roots will clog the pump filter, so only use potted plants, or plan to build some sort of additional screen or filtration system. A pump that moves 120 gallons per hour is plenty big enough for this situation.

Now it's time to fill up your new creation with water and plants. If the local nursery doesn't carry water plants, you can order them online.

Figure A Patio pond

Overall dimensions: 66-3/4" x 21" x 15-1/2"

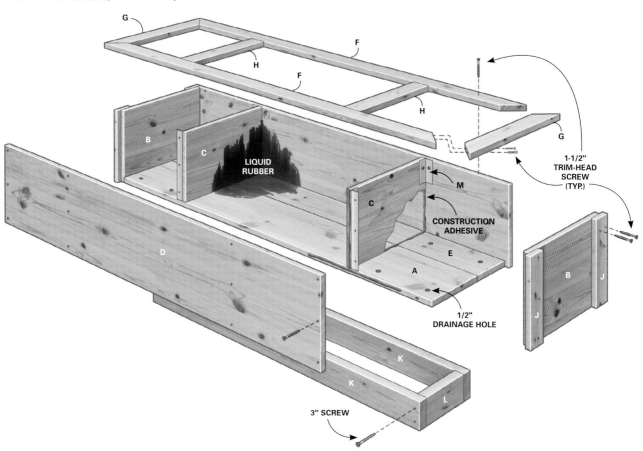

Cutting list

KEY	DIMENSIONS	QTY.	NAME
Cut from rough-sawn 1x12 cedar*			
A	62-1/4" x 11-1/4" x 7/8"	1	Bottom
B	16-3/4" x 11-1/4" x 7/8"	2	Ends
C	16-3/4" x 10-3/8" x 7/8"	2	Dividers
D	64" x 11-1/4" x 7/8"	2	Sides
*Widths may vary			
Cut from 1x6 rough-sawn cedar			
E	62-1/4" x 5-1/2" x 7/8"	1	Bottom
F	2-11/16" x 66-3/4" x 7/8"	2	Face frame sides
G	2-11/16" x 21" x 7/8"	2	Face frame ends
H	2-11/16" x 15-9/16"	2	Face frame dividers
J	2-11/16" x 11-1/4"	4	End caps
Cedar-tone pressure-treated 2x4			
K	54" x 3-1/2" x 1-1/2"	2	Base sides
L	8-1/2" x 3-1/2" x 1-1/2"	2	Base ends
Aluminum angle stock			
M	10-1/4" x 1-1/4" x 1/16"	4	Corner bracket

Materials list

ITEM	QTY.
1x12 x 12' rough-sawn cedar	2
1x6 x 8' rough-sawn cedar	3
2x4 x 12' cedar-tone pressure-treated lumber	1
1-1/4" x 1/16" x 4' aluminum angle stock	1
Small box of 1-1/2" exterior trim-head screws	1
Small box of 1-1/4" drywall or cabinet screws	1
Small box of 3" screws compatible with pressure-treated lumber	1
Small box of 3/4" screws	1
Tube of construction adhesive	1
Gallon of liquid rubber	

7 GARDEN FEATURES

Easy garden arch

A small project that makes a big impression in your backyard

Building an arch is one of the easiest ways to give your landscape a striking centerpiece. And this arch is easier than most. Made from just six parts, it can be built in less than a day—even if you're a rookie carpenter. The design is versatile, too: The arch can become a gateway in a fence, frame a walkway through a hedge or stand alone in your yard or garden. You can stain it for a rustic look or paint it for a more formal look.

Money and materials

The total materials bill for the cedar arch shown here was a couple hundred dollars. Built from pressure-treated lumber, it would cost about half that. Depending on where you live, you may have other choices of rot-resistant lumber available, such as cypress or redwood. If you choose treated lumber, you'll find everything you need for this project at home

WHAT IT TAKES

TIME: 1 day

SKILL LEVEL: Beginner to intermediate

centers. If you choose another wood species, you may have to special-order lumber or visit a traditional lumberyard.

You'll need only standard tools like a drill, a circular saw and a jigsaw. Make sure your framing square is a standard model (16 x 24 in., with a longer leg that's 2 in. wide). If yours is an oddball, buy a standard version so you can easily mark out the brackets (see Photo 2). A few days before you dig the postholes, call 811 to have underground utility lines marked.

Cut the parts

To get started, cut notches in the tops of the posts (Photo 1). If you're using "rough-sawn" lumber as we did, you may have to change the length and depth of these notches to suit your 2x8 headers. (The dimensions of rough-sawn lumber vary.) Set the cutting depth of your circular saw to 1-1/2 in. to make the crosscuts for the notches. Then set your saw to full depth to make the other cuts.

Next cut the 2x8 headers to length and mark arcs at the ends as shown in Figure A. To mark the curves, use the bottom of a 5-gallon bucket or any circle that's 10 to 11 in. in diameter. Cut the curves with a jigsaw.

The curved brackets may look complicated, but they're easy to mark since they're based on a standard framing square. After marking with the square (Photo 2), set a nail in your sawhorse 20 in. from the edge of the board. Carefully adjust the position of the board until both corner marks of the bracket are 24 in. from the nail. Then, holding your pencil at the 24-in. mark on the tape, draw an arc. To draw the second arc, move your pencil to the 29-in. mark on the tape (Photo 3). Cut the straight edges of the brackets with a circular saw and the arcs with a jigsaw. If the curves turn out a bit wavy, smooth them with an orbital or belt sander. Don't be too fussy, though. Nobody will notice small imperfections.

Put it all together

Mark one header 12 in. from both ends and lay out the posts, aligned with the marks. Take measurements at the other end to make sure the posts are perfectly parallel. Drive 3-1/2-in. screws through the posts and into the header. At the tops of the brackets, drive 3-in. screws at a slight angle so they won't poke through the face of the header (Photo 4). Set 1-1/2-in.-thick blocks under the other ends of the brackets. Then drive screws at an angle through the sides of the brackets and into the posts. Be sure to drill 1/8-in. pilot holes so you don't split the brackets. Set the second header in place and screw it to the posts. Note: The brackets are not centered on the posts, so there's a 1-in. gap between the second header and the brackets.

Set it up

You'll set the arch posts into 10-in.-diameter holes 30 in. deep. But before you move the arch into place, screw on a temporary 2x4 "stretcher" 30 in. from the post bottoms. Then round up a helper or two and set the posts into the holes. Patiently level and plumb the arch, using stakes and 2x4s to brace it (Photo 5). Be careful not to nudge the posts out of position as you fill the holes with concrete. Let the concrete harden for at least four hours before you finish the wood. Brush on two coats of clear penetrating wood finish to deepen the color of the wood and repel moisture.

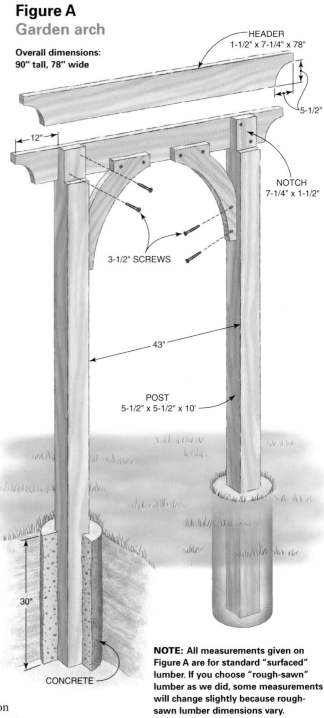

Figure A
Garden arch

Overall dimensions:
90" tall, 78" wide

HEADER
1-1/2" x 7-1/4" x 78"

5-1/2"

12"

NOTCH
7-1/4" x 1-1/2"

3-1/2" SCREWS

43"

POST
5-1/2" x 5-1/2" x 10'

30"

CONCRETE

NOTE: All measurements given on Figure A are for standard "surfaced" lumber. If you choose "rough-sawn" lumber as we did, some measurements will change slightly because rough-sawn lumber dimensions vary.

Materials list

ITEM	QTY.
6x6 x 10' (posts)	2
2x8 x 8' (headers)	2
2x10 x 8' (brackets)	1
2x4 x 8' (stretcher, stakes, braces)	3
Concrete mix (60-lb. bags)	3
3" and 3-1/2" screws	

1 Notch the tops of the posts. Cut as deep as you can from both sides with a circular saw, then finish the cuts with a handsaw.

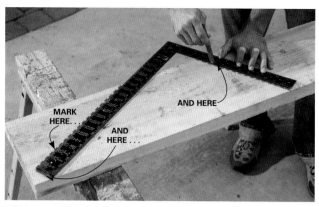

2 Mark the brackets without fussy measurements or geometry—just align a framing square with the edges of a 2x10 and make three marks.

MARK HERE...
AND HERE
AND HERE...

3 Draw perfect curves fast using a tape measure to guide your pencil. Cut out the bracket and use it as a pattern for the other bracket.

BRACKET
HEADER

4 Screw through the posts and brackets into the header. That way, one header will have no visible screws. Screw through the second header into the posts.

STRETCHER
SHIMS

5 Set the arch level and plumb before you pour concrete into the postholes. Wedge shims under the stretcher until the header is level, then plumb and brace the posts.

Figure B
Bracket detail

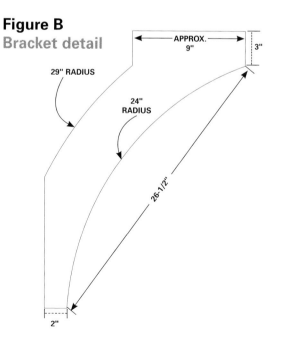

APPROX. 9"
3"
29" RADIUS
24" RADIUS
26-1/2"
2"

Pyramid trellis

A 7-foot trellis that's a cinch to build

Y ou would pay a bundle for a trellis like this at a garden center—or you can build it in an afternoon for less than half the retail price. If you use pressure-treated wood, the trellis will last a long time and never need a coat of stain.

How to build it

1. From four 2x2s, cut four 84-in.-long legs. Cut at 90 degrees.
2. Cut horizontal spacers from the remaining 2x2s. All of these pieces should be cut at 6 degrees, with the angles opposing. Cut four pieces each to these lengths (length given is for the widest side of the piece): 18-1/2 in.; 13-1/8 in.; 8-3/8 in.; and 4-1/8 in.
3. Rip just enough wood from the two 6-ft. 5/4-in. x 6-in. deck boards to eliminate both rounded edges. Then rip the boards 1-1/8 in. wide—you'll get four pieces from each board. From these, cut four pieces 60 in. long and eight pieces 36 in. long. Cut two 45-degree angles on one end of each to make a decorative peak.
4. Measure and mark positions of the four spacers on the legs. To do this, lay all four legs together, with sides touching and tops and bottoms aligned. Measure and mark as shown in Figure B. Work from the bottom up. Set aside two of the legs.
5. Lay the other two legs on your workbench, with their sides touching. Keep the legs together at the tops (a heavy-duty rubber band around the tops will help) while spreading them apart at the bottom. Center the longest spacer at the lowest mark on the legs, the second-longest spacer at the second mark, and so on.

   Fasten the spacers using 2-1/2-in. screws (drill pilot holes first).Start at the bottom and work your way up. As you screw the spacer to one leg, clamp the other down or nail a board behind it on your bench so you have something to push against. When positioning these screws, leave room for the screws you'll use to attach adjacent spacers (see Detail illustration). Assemble the other set of legs the same way.
6. Stand the two sets of legs upright on a level floor, with the tops touching. Spread the bottom legs to make room for the spacers that hold the two sets together. Hold the tops together temporarily by wrapping with duct tape.

   Drill a pilot hole and fasten the longest spacer between the sets with a 2-1/2-in. screw to one side. (Take care not to hit the screw on the adjacent side.) Next, attach the shortest spacer on the same side. Fasten the second and third spacers last. Attach spacers on the opposite side in the same order.
7. Make a 4-1/2-in.-square finial platform from a 2-in. x 6-in. scrap of pressure-treated lumber. (You can find these pieces in the scrap bin at most building centers for a small fee.) Rip the piece to 4-1/2 in. first, then cut a piece 4-1/2 in. long from the board.
8. Find the center point of the platform by drawing lines that connect the opposite corners with a straight edge. Mark the center where the lines

Materials list

Note: Use pressure-treated lumber.

6 2" x 2" x 8'

2 5/4 x 6" x 6' deck boards

1 2" x 6" x 6" board

1 3/16" x 2-1/2" dowel screw

   3-1/2", 2-1/2", 2" and 1-5/8" galvanized deck screws

1 decorative finial

Tools

■ Table saw

■ Power drill

■ Duct tape

Figure A
Pyramid trellis

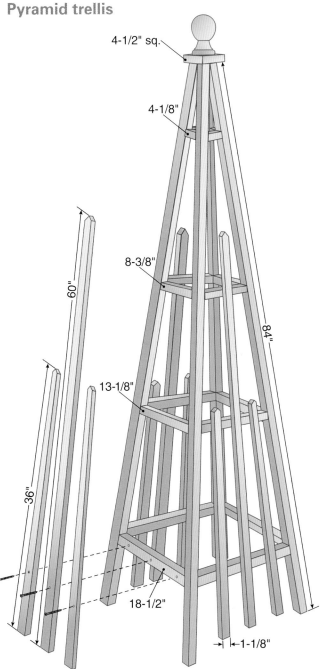

- 4-1/2" sq.
- 4-1/8"
- 8-3/8"
- 60"
- 13-1/8"
- 84"
- 36"
- 18-1/2"
- 1-1/8"

intersect with an awl. Predrill a hole for the 3/16-in. dowel screw (also called a double-ended wood screw) in the spot you've marked. Sand the platform for a rounded appearance.

9. Attach the platform to the legs. Predrill holes on the platform for 3-1/2-in. screws. Angle the holes so they run parallel to the legs. Screw the platform into the top ends of the legs.

   Attach a dowel screw for the finial in the center of the platform, then thread a decorative finial onto the screw.

10. Center the longest vertical "spear" on each side, drill pilot holes and attach to the spacers with 1-5/8-in. deck screws. Center short spears between the legs and the long spears, then fasten to the spacers with deck screws. The bottom of each spear should be about 1 in. off the ground. This will ensure that the trellis rests on the legs instead of the spears.

    If you plan to use the trellis in a windy spot, you may want to anchor it. Drive two pipes into the ground, then attach the trellis to them with cable ties or hose clamps.

    Remove the duct tape and plant some vining flowers.

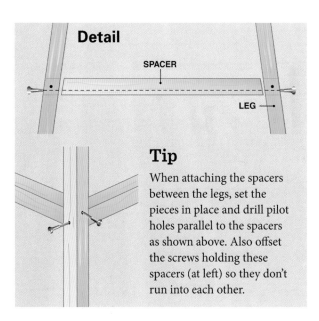

Detail

SPACER

LEG

Tip

When attaching the spacers between the legs, set the pieces in place and drill pilot holes parallel to the spacers as shown above. Also offset the screws holding these spacers (at left) so they don't run into each other.

Figure B
Spacer locations

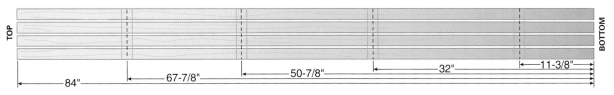

TOP — BOTTOM

84" — 67-7/8" — 50-7/8" — 32" — 11-3/8"

Lay legs together and mark. These are the centers where the spacers will attach.

Copper wire trellis

A garden project with a twist

WHAT IT TAKES

TIME: 1 day
SKILL LEVEL: Beginner to intermediate

The first reaction of most people when they see this trellis is, "Wow! I love it!" The second reaction is, "How in the world did you make it?"

Well, there's a trick to bending the wire, that's for sure, but once you understand it, this trellis goes together pretty easily. When you're done, you've got an elegant garden ornament that looks great even when the plants that climb on it have died back.

Give it a year or two outdoors and the wood will turn gray and the copper will turn a beautiful dark brown, and then eventually green. It wouldn't be hard to customize this trellis, forming the copper wire into initials or even more fanciful shapes.

Materials and tools

The copper scrollwork is made from No. 6 solid-copper wire, which is used for grounding electrical panels and is available at most home centers. This wire is stiff enough to hold its shape on the trellis, but soft enough to bend easily. The rest of the trellis is made from 2x2s and 1/2-in. copper pipe.

In the tool department, you'll need a drill and a 5/8-in. spade bit, a pair of medium to large wire-cutting pliers (test them out on the copper wire to see if they can cut it), a miter box or electric miter saw and an electric sander.

Make the trellis from treated lumber, or spend a bit more and use clear cedar, shown here.

Begin with the legs and rungs

Begin with the four legs, the wooden center posts and the copper pipe rungs that connect them.

1. Place your four 2x2 legs on sawhorses, get the top ends even and clamp them all together.
2. Mark one end as the top, and measure from that end at 28 in., 41-1/2 in. and 59 in. to mark where you will drill the holes. Use a square to transfer the marks to all four legs and to the adjacent side of one leg.
3. Make an angle guide by cutting a piece of scrap wood at an 80-degree angle (Photo 1). An inexpensive protractor works fine to set the angle.
4. Drill angled holes at each mark, using your guide, so you're drilling three holes in each leg (Photo 1). Mark your drill bit to indicate the 1-in. depth for the holes, and be sure the drill is always leaning toward the top of the legs.
5. Flip each leg 90 degrees, clamp them together and repeat the whole process. The marks you made on the second side of one leg will allow you to transfer your hole locations. Be careful—the drill may be a bit jumpy as the second hole meets the first.
6. Cut six pieces of pipe (C, D and E) as shown in Photo 2, inset. Note in the Cutting List (on p. 104) that there are two sets of

pipe rungs; one set is slightly longer. Cut the longer set now.
7. Temporarily assemble one side of the trellis—two legs and three pieces of pipe. Tap the legs to get the pipe seated. The tops of the legs should be within 1/4 in. of each other.
8. Cut the center posts (B) to length, and use a miter box or miter saw to cut points on the ends. A line marked around all four sides will help guide you.
9. Lay the center post on top of the assembled side. Be sure the post is centered and equidistant from the legs. Mark the post

1 Drill holes in the legs using a wood scrap cut at 80 degrees to guide you. With all four legs clamped together, it's easy to get the holes to line up.

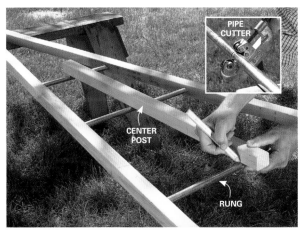

2 Lay a center post on the rungs, which are cut from copper pipe, and mark the rung holes directly on the post. Be sure the post is centered top-to-bottom and side-to-side.

3 Your bending jig for the wire scrolls is a piece of scrap wood with a copy of the scroll pattern (p. 104) tacked to it. Two finish nails in the middle hold the pieces of copper wire.

4 Bend the scrolls with your hands, following the pattern. The copper wire is soft enough to bend easily. When you've bent one side, weight it down and bend the other.

Figure A
Copper wire trellis

For clarity, only one
of four sides is shown.

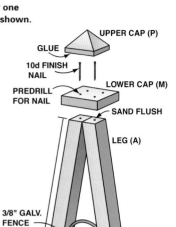

UPPER CAP (P)

GLUE

10d FINISH
NAIL

PREDRILL
FOR NAIL

LOWER CAP (M)

SAND FLUSH

LEG (A)

3/8" GALV.
FENCE
STAPLE

45°

28"

UPPER PIPE RUNG (C)

41-1/2"

MIDDLE
PIPE RUNG
(D)

SCROLL

59"

5/8" DIA.
1" DEEP
10°

CENTER
POST (B)

LOWER
PIPE RUNG
(E)

BURY A
FEW INCHES
IN THE GROUND

Figure B
Lower scroll

Enlarge to an overall
length of 16-3/4"

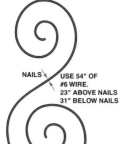

NAILS

USE 54" OF
#6 WIRE.
23" ABOVE NAILS
31" BELOW NAILS

Figure C
Middle scroll

Enlarge to an overall
length of 12-3/4"

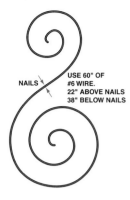

NAILS

USE 60" OF
#6 WIRE.
22" ABOVE NAILS
38" BELOW NAILS

Figure D
Upper scroll

Enlarge to an overall
length of 13-3/4"

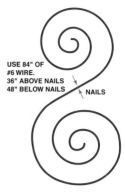

USE 84" OF
#6 WIRE.
36" ABOVE NAILS
48" BELOW NAILS

NAILS

Materials list

6   2x2 x 8'
1   4x4 x 1'
1   1x6 x 1'
115' of #6 solid-copper wire
16' of 1/2" copper pipe
One box fence staples
Six 10d finish nails
One tube construction adhesive

Cutting list
Overall Dimensions: 69"H x 26"W x 26"D

KEY	NAME	QTY.	DIMENSIONS
A	leg	4	1-1/2" x 1-1/2" x 72"
B	center post	4	1-1/2" x 1-1/2" x 35-1/2"
C	upper pipe	2	1/2" dia. x 11-1/4"
D	middle pipe	2	1/2" dia. x 15-3/4"
E	lower pipe	2	1/2" dia. x 21-3/4"
F	upper pipe	2	1/2" dia. x 10-3/4"
G	middle pipe	2	1/2" dia. x 15-1/4"
H	lower pipe	2	1/2" dia. x 21-1/4"
J	upper scroll	4	#6 wire x 60"
K	middle scroll	8	#6 wire x 54"
L	lower scroll	8	#6 wire x 84"
M	lower cap	1	3/4" x 4" x 4"
P	upper cap	1	3-1/2" x 3-1/2" x 2-1/4"

5 Attach the scrolls with small fence staples. You can bend the scroll out of the way temporarily to make room for the hammer.

6 Sand the top where all four legs come together, using coarse sandpaper, so they form a flat surface for nailing on the cap.

for the pipe holes, then transfer the marks to the other three center posts and drill the holes at 90 degrees. Drill from one side until the point of the spade bit pokes through, then drill the other side. This gives you cleaner holes.

Be careful inserting the pipe

10. Assemble two sides. Put the pipes through the center posts, get them centered, then place the ends of the pipes in the legs. Be careful as you insert the pipe in the center post. It's possible to split out a chunk of the wood as the pipe exits the post. When you're done, the tops of the legs should be within 1/4 in. of each other.

11. Lay an assembled side upside down on sawhorses so the remaining holes in the legs are pointing up and supported. Using a bolt, an old screwdriver or similar tool, mash the end of the pipe where you can see it at the bottom of each hole. This will lock the pipe in place and make room at the bottom of the hole for the other pipes.

12. Cut the remaining pipe rungs (F, G and H) and then fit the rungs and remaining center posts between the two assembled sides to form the complete trellis structure. If any of the joints are loose, put a bit of epoxy in the hole.

Bend the scrolls

Now the fun part: making the wire scrollwork.

13. Make your bending jig out of a 2x12 or a scrap piece of plywood at least 11 in. x 18 in. Enlarge the patterns in Figures B, C and D until the dimensions are correct, and tack a pattern to the jig (Photo 3). Nail two 10d finish nails on either side of the scroll shape to hold the wire (see Figures B, C and D).

14. Cut one piece of wire to the appropriate length for the scroll you're working on. Measure from one end to find the point that goes between the two finish nails (see pattern drawing), mark that spot and lay the wire on the jig so your mark is between the two nails. Using your hand only,

bend the wire to the shape on the pattern (Photo 4). There should be a few inches of extra wire on each end to give you something to hold. When you've got the first half bent to shape, snip the end. Put a weight or a clamp on the part you've done, then bend the other side. You don't have to be fussy about matching the pattern; close is good enough.

15. If your first scroll was a success, cut the remaining pieces of wire and bend the rest of the scrolls. For each of the three different shapes, do one for practice before cutting the remaining wire. If you have trouble, cut the wire a little long and you'll have more to work with.

Final assembly

16. Lay the trellis on its side and use fence staples to attach the scrolls to the 2x2s (Photo 5). Be sure to get the pairs of scrolls on each side of the trellis to be symmetrical (a right and a left), and to reverse the direction between the lower and middle scrolls (see Figure A).

17. When all the scrolls are attached, stand the trellis up, find yourself something to stand on, and sand the tops of the legs flat and even (Photo 6). If the pieces vibrate too much, tape them all together with duct tape or packing tape.

18. Cut the cap pieces (M and P). For the facets on the topmost cap piece (P), start with a 1-ft.-long piece of 4x4 so you have enough wood to hold on to while you cut the facets. Then trim off the finished cap piece. You can also buy deck caps at a home center to avoid the cutting completely. When both cap pieces are cut, drill pilot holes in M, nail it on, then glue on part P with construction adhesive or epoxy.

19. Install the trellis in your garden. Dig the bottoms of the legs into the earth and get the trellis plumb. You'll have to do it pretty much by eye. If your location is windy, anchor the bottoms of the legs into the ground. One way is to bend a couple of 3-ft. pieces of 1/8-in. rod into a U-shape, so they can be driven in around the legs. Then fasten them to the legs with fence staples and cover with dirt or mulch.

Entry arbors & trellis

WHAT IT TAKES

TIME: 1 weekend
SKILL LEVEL: Intermediate

Use this simple, versatile design to frame your walk, screen bland walls and decorate with ivy

You don't have to hire an architect to redesign your front entry to make it attractive and inviting. Sometimes a simple, inexpensive arbor or trellis will do the trick. This home featured a pretty brick facing . . . flanked by a big blank vinyl-sided wall that begged for screening. Our solution was to hide it behind a simple trellis. An even simpler version of the same design is used to frame an arbor that borders the sidewalk on both sides. This feature not only beautifies the

entry but also guides guests to the front door.

Here, we'll show you a simple technique that'll allow you to build both projects. Photos 1 – 7 demonstrate the building of the open-sided arbors. Photos 8 – 10 show how to assemble the trellis. This truly is a relaxed weekend project. You just need to be able to dig a few holes and operate a circular saw and a screw gun. You cut and assemble everything in place, so it's easy to measure and cut the pieces to fit as you go.

1 Stake the post positions using a rectangular 2x4 template. Remove the template and dig the postholes.

2 Screw the lower post assemblies together with four pairs of screws on each side (Figure A).

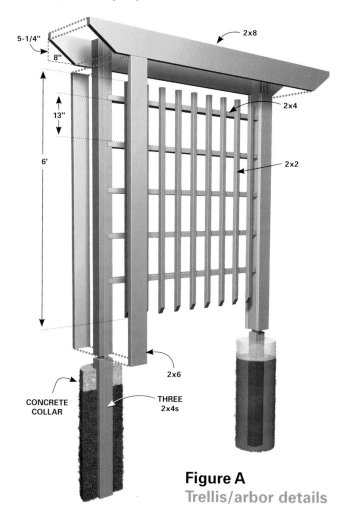

Figure A
Trellis/arbor details

Labels: 5-1/4", 8", 13", 6', 2x8, 2x4, 2x2, 2x6, CONCRETE COLLAR, THREE 2x4s

4', 3" DECK SCREWS, 2x4 x 12' POST CENTER

3 Drop the posts into their postholes, then plumb them both ways and toe-screw them to the template. Tamp soil around it to brace it.

2x4 and 2x6 "sandwich" posts simplify assembly

The bottom portions of the posts are made from three treated 2x4s to keep the dirt-bound parts from rotting. The center 2x4 is continuous to keep the posts strong, but we cut the outside 2x4s off just above grade so we could transition to better-looking cedar. We chose cedar for its natural rot resistance, its ability to hold paint and its stability. If cedar isn't available in your area, use any naturally rot-resistant wood that's available for the above-grade wood. Redwood and cypress are excellent substitutes. If you want to save, you could even use common construction-grade lumber. If you paint all sides and the cut ends before assembly, the project will last for years. Or build it entirely with treated wood. But keep in mind that treated wood is often of low quality and has a tendency to warp, twist and crack. It may not be as handsome down the road as other choices. And you also may have to wait weeks for the treated wood to dry well enough to hold paint.

LONG 2x4

SHORT 2x4s

4 Mark the short side posts a few inches above grade and cut them off with a circular saw. Take care not to cut the long center post.

CUT MARK

2x8 LINTEL

TEMPORARY BLOCK

5 Cut the lintels to length, then level and rest them on temporary blocks. Mark the height of the center 2x4s, then cut them off with your circular saw.

We designed the trellis grid work with close spacing to support climbing plants. You can make your grid work with larger spaces, or tighter if the trellis alone will be the screen, without vines. We fastened the grid work high enough above the patio to allow space for a planter box below. If you're building the grid work to look like ours, get five cedar 2x4 "rungs" (horizontal members; Figure A) long enough to span between posts. Also pick up three 8-ft.-long 2x2 pickets (verticals) for each foot of width, or rip them from 2x4s.

Build a template and dig the postholes

A 2x4 template makes quick work of marking accurate post positions and of setting the posts (Photo 1). Decide on the best footprint for the arbors and make the template dimensions to match the corners of the posts. Be sure to square up your template by matching diagonal measurements (distances between opposite corners should be the same) and then add a brace to keep it square. Use screws for fasteners so you can take the template apart easily after you're through setting the posts.

Drive stakes into the ground at the corners to mark the holes and then set aside the template. Dig 8-in.-wide holes about 3 ft. deep and pack the bottom of

each hole with a shovel handle so the posts won't settle later. After the holes are dug, return the template to the same spot for setting the posts.

The template helps keep the posts plumb and aligned. Push the preassembled posts against the template and plumb each post in both directions. Toe-screw each one to the template to hold it plumb while you fill in the hole with soil (Photo 3). If the template moves around too much, just anchor it to the ground with a few temporary stakes.

Use a single 2x4 for a template when you're setting the two posts for the trellis. Make sure the posts lie flat against the 2x4 to ensure that the post sides remain aligned. After plumbing each post

Materials list

Treated wood: For each post, you'll need a treated 12-ft.-long 2x4 for the center and an 8-ft.-long treated 2x4 cut in half for the shorter post sides (Photo 2).

Cedar: For wrapping each post, buy two 8-ft. cedar 2x4s and two 8-ft. 2x6s. Also buy two 2x8 cedar lintel boards at least 3 ft. longer than the distance between the posts (outside-to-outside dimension).

Hardware: Buy a 1-lb. box of 3-in. deck screws for joining all of the components except the pickets. Buy a 1-lb. box of 10d galvanized finish nails for that job. And get one 60-lb. bag of premixed concrete for each pair of posts.

with a level, add fill, packing it as you go. Fill the top 8 in. with concrete. If you're going to quit for the day, mix the concrete now and collar each post with a half bag (60-lb. bags). Otherwise, go on to the next step, adding the cedar trim, and add the concrete later.

Assemble the cedar parts

Start by cutting off the short treated 2x4s a couple of inches above the final grade (Photo 4). Be sure to account for the finished height, including sod, pavers or mulch. The idea is to keep the cedar above the ground to prevent rot.

Cut the 2x8 lintels to length and cut the decorative angles on the ends (Figure A). Support one of the leveled 2x8 lintels on temporary blocks at the desired height to mark the top of the center 2x4 for trimming (Photo 5). Before you take the 2x8 down, use a level and a long straightedge to transfer the post height to the posts on the opposite arbor. That way the arbor tops will match.

Installing the cedar cladding is simple; it's just a matter of measuring, cutting and screwing the parts together. Photos 6 and 7 show you how.

If you're building a trellis next to a wall as we did, you may not be able to fit a screw gun between the wall and the trellis to drive the screws. If so, just toe-screw those parts from the front.

Tip

You'll save tons of time by painting or sealing the cedar parts before assembly. You'll still have freshly cut ends to touch up, but that only takes moments.

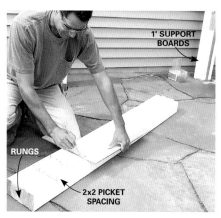

1' SUPPORT BOARDS

RUNGS

2x2 PICKET SPACING

6 Cut the cedar 2x4 post trim boards to length and screw them to the center treated post. Then screw the lintels in place flush with the post top.

2x4 TRIM

7 Cut the 2x6 post trim to fit directly under the lintel and screw it to the cedar 2x4s, keeping an even overhang on both sides.

2x6 TRIM

8 Set the trellis posts, then cut the 2x4 rungs to fit between them. Cluster the rungs and lay out the picket positions.

VERTICAL-SUPPORT

9 Stack the rungs over the vertical supports, screwing each one to the tops below it as you work. You'll cover the joints with 2x6s later.

GUIDE BOARD

2x6 TRIM

10 Tack a level guide board across the posts. Push the pickets against the guide and nail them to each rung with 10d finish nails. Add the last 2x6 trim boards.

Install the trellis grid work

Assemble the trellis exactly the same as the arbor, except leave off the 2x4 post trim on the inside of the posts as well as the outside 2x6 (Photo 9). Cut the horizontal rungs to fit between the posts and work out your picket spacing on one of them. This takes a bit of figuring; allow for the thickness of the inside 2x4 trim and try for even spacing. Or simply position a picket in the center and work out in both directions. Once you have the right pattern, transfer the layout to all of the horizontal rungs (Photo 8).

Photo 9 and Figure A show you the correct assembly order and the spacing we used for the rungs and pickets. Start with the bottom 2x4 blocks, screw a rung to the tops, then another block, another rung and so on. Cut 45-degree angles on the picket ends for a more decorative look if you choose. Tack up a temporary guide board parallel to the lintel to help align the pickets as you nail them up. That'll keep them straight.

8 GARDEN TOOLS & EQUIPMENT

Build a compost bin

This "log cabin" bin will keep your compost pile from becoming an eyesore

Why not turn your yard waste into yard gold by building this compost bin? Build it now, then start your compost pile with leaves, garden plants and some grass clippings. (Leave most of the clippings on the lawn to return nitrogen to the grass as they decompose.)

You probably already own all the tools you'll need. Round up a circular saw, a coping saw, a tape measure, a drill/driver, 1/16-in.-dia. and 3/8-in.-dia. drill bits, a carpenter's square, two pipe clamps and a wood chisel.

The bin is constructed from "five-quarter" (5/4) rounded-edge decking boards. (Although the name implies that these are 1-1/4 in. boards, they're actually only about 1 in. thick.) The boards are pressure-treated, which makes the bin resistant to rot and insects. There's very little hardware because the pieces fit together like classic Lincoln Logs.

Cutting the pieces

All of the 5/4 decking needs to be cut to 42-in. lengths—you'll get four 42-in. boards from each 14-ft. board. (Hauling 14-ft. boards can be a hassle, so have the lumberyard cut each one into two 7-footers.) The 42-in. boards, when assembled, give you a compost bin that's approximately a 3-ft. cube.

Two of the 42-in. boards will need to be ripped in half (cut down their length). Two of the ripped pieces (parts D) need to be cut to 2-3/8 in. wide and then notched (see Figure A). One of the pieces should be cut to 1-1/2 in. wide (part C). The remaining piece is scrap, which you'll use later.

Cutting treated lumber requires special precautions. Here's what to do:
- Wear a dust mask to avoid inhaling the sawdust.
- Do the cutting outdoors.
- Clean up scraps and throw them in the trash. DO NOT burn treated lumber. It gives off toxic fumes!
- Wash exposed skin after cutting the lumber.

Notching the boards

Interlocking, 1-3/16 in. deep notches hold the bin together. Notches cut to this depth leave about a 3/4-in. space between each pair of boards when interlocked. The exact width of the notches depends on the thickness of the lumber, but remember, 5/4 lumber is actually only about 1 in. thick.

Here's how to cut the notches:
- Clamp the like components together with pipe clamps. Then stand them on edge on a solid work surface (Photo 1). Not all the pieces require the same number of notches; check Figure A for the number required for each component.
- Measure in from the edge of the boards 1-3/4 in. and draw a line at this distance on all of the boards. Now, measure from this line 1 in. (or the thickness of your lumber) toward the center of the boards and draw a second line.

Figure A
Compost bin

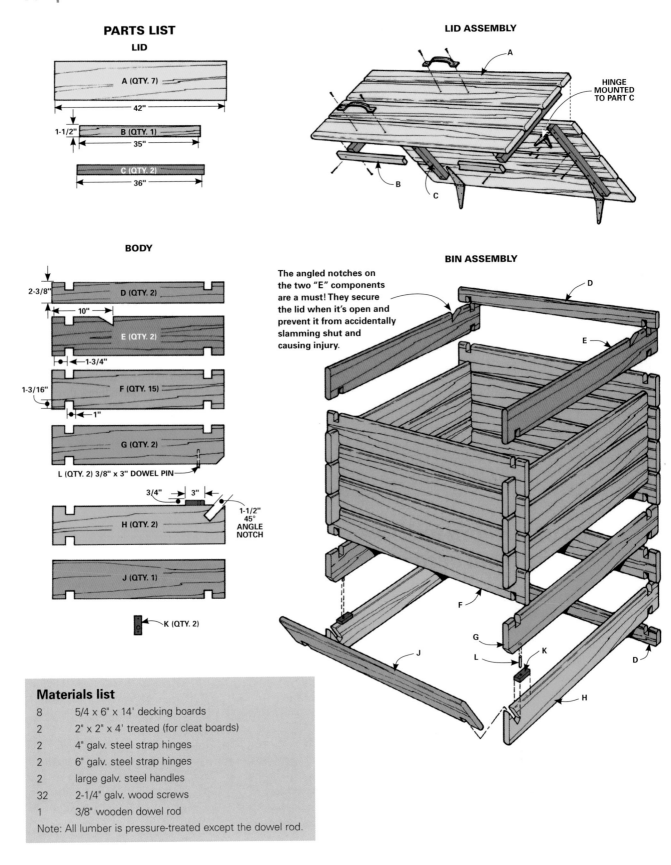

PARTS LIST
LID

A (QTY. 7)
42"
1-1/2"
B (QTY. 1)
35"
C (QTY. 2)
36"

LID ASSEMBLY

A

HINGE MOUNTED TO PART C

B
C

BODY

2-3/8"
D (QTY. 2)
10"
E (QTY. 2)
1-3/4"
1-3/16"
F (QTY. 15)
1"
G (QTY. 2)
L (QTY. 2) 3/8" x 3" DOWEL PIN
3/4"   3"
1-1/2" 45° ANGLE NOTCH
H (QTY. 2)
J (QTY. 1)
K (QTY. 2)

BIN ASSEMBLY

The angled notches on the two "E" components are a must! They secure the lid when it's open and prevent it from accidentally slamming shut and causing injury.

D
E
F
G
J
L
K
D
H

Materials list

8	5/4 x 6" x 14' decking boards
2	2" x 2" x 4' treated (for cleat boards)
2	4" galv. steel strap hinges
2	6" galv. steel strap hinges
2	large galv. steel handles
32	2-1/4" galv. wood screws
1	3/8" wooden dowel rod

Note: All lumber is pressure-treated except the dowel rod.

1 Clamp the like components together with pipe clamps on both ends. Use a circular saw to cut 1/4-in.-wide slices to make the 1-in.-wide, 1-3/16-in.-deep notches.

2 Remove the slices with a wood chisel. Use a coping saw to square the corners of the notches to make a tight-fitting joint.

- Set your circular saw to cut at a depth of 1-3/16 in. and cut along the entire length of both lines. Now make a series of 1/4-in.-wide cuts or slices (Photo 1).
- Remove the slices with a wood chisel (Photo 2). Square the bottom corners of each notch with a chisel for tight-fitting corners.

After you finish the interlocking notches, cut the 45-degree diagonal notches in the two bottom side boards (parts H). The cuts can be started with the circular saw, but finish them with a coping saw.

Next, cut two 3/4-in.-thick, 3-in.-long spacer blocks (parts K) from the scrap lumber. Drill a 1/16-in.-dia. hole through

What to compost

- Green plant material (the nitrogen supply) with brown materials such as fall leaves (the carbon supply).
- Any plant materials (except weeds with seeds and poisonous plants such as poison ivy), straw, coffee grounds, eggshells (not the whole egg), and raw fruit and vegetable scraps. Do NOT compost meat, dairy products or pet feces.

Starting the pile

The pile needs to be built in layers. The bottom layer should be 8 to 10 in. of an even mix of grass and leaves or other plant trimmings.

Water this layer so that it's moist, but not soggy. You can add a 1-in. layer of soil over the nitrogen-rich plant matter to increase the number of decomposing microorganisms.

Repeat these layers until the pile fills the bin.

each end of each spacer and a 3/8-in.-dia. hole in the center of the spacer. Then nail the spacers to the bottom side boards (parts H).

Measure from the front edge of parts H to the center of the 3/8-in. hole in the spacer. Mark this measurement on the bottom front of the part G boards and drill a 1-1/4 in.-deep, 3/8-in.-dia. hole for the dowel (L).

Cut two, 3-in. lengths of 3/8-in.-dia. dowel and tap them into the holes through the spacers.

Now you're ready to assemble the other components Lincoln Log style. First, move all of the components to the bin site before you start. The bin's not easy to move once it's fully assembled.

Constructing the top

Building the lid is quick and easy. Here's how:
- Lay out the seven remaining 42-in. boards, making sure they're tight together, edge to edge.
- Measure in 3-1/2 in. from both ends and mark. This is where you'll attach the 2 x 2-in. cleats (C). Use 2-1/4-in. galvanized wood screws.

Don't put screws into the cleat board that's directly over the center of the top's middle board. Now rip the center board in half to form the two lid sections. Cut completely through the cleat board when you rip the center board.
- Connect the two lid sections with 4-in. strap hinges using the screws that come with the hinges.
- Mount one leaf of the 6-in. strap hinges (they secure the lid to the bin) just inside the cleat boards. Mount the other leaf on the outside of the back of the bin.
- Finally, attach the handles as shown in the illustration on p. 112.

Cedar potting bench

Build this handy potting bench in a weekend

SOLID NOTCHED JOINTS

GRATE-COVERED DIRT CATCHER

BUILT-IN POTTING SOIL CONTAINER

REMOVABLE CONTAINER COVER

WHAT IT TAKES

TIME: 1 weekend

SKILL LEVEL: Intermediate

Whether you're a spare-time gardener or a hard-core enthusiast, this bench is for you. It has plenty of storage to keep all your plant supplies in one convenient location, and it features a built-in potting soil container and a grate-covered dirt catcher to make messy potting and cleanup a snap.

Here you'll learn how to build this cedar potting bench in a weekend.

This bench was designed to be strong without complex joints. An experienced woodworker can complete this potting bench in a day. If you're a beginner, allow two or three days.

You'll need basic carpentry tools like a tape measure, large and small squares, and a chisel. You could make most of the cuts for this potting bench with a circular saw. However, a power miter saw will ensure perfectly square end cuts, and a table saw is almost essential for cutting the grate slats. If you don't have a table saw, ask a friend, neighbor or the staff at the lumberyard to cut the pieces for you. You'll also need a drill with the bits mentioned here, and a jigsaw.

Choose straight, nice-looking lumber

Use the Materials List below to buy your materials. Shown is cedar, but pine is cheaper. Consider using pressure-treated pine if you'll be leaving the bench outside. All of these are available at home centers and lumberyards.

Make tight-fitting joints for a strong bench

Photos 1 and 2 show how to notch the legs for the horizontal cross members. Notching looks tricky, but it's simple if you follow these key steps: First clamp each pair of legs together, and using dimensions from Figure A, mark the lower edge of each notch. Use a square to draw lines across the boards at these marks. Then align the corresponding horizontal board with this line and mark along the opposite edge to get an exact width. Using the boards in this manner to mark the width of the notch is more accurate than measuring. When you saw the notch, cut to the waste side of the pencil line, leaving the line on the board. You can always enlarge the notch or plane the board to fit a notch that's too tight, but you can't shrink a notch that's too wide. Tight-fitting joints strengthen the bench and look better too.

Assembly is quick once the parts are cut

Photos 3 and 4 show how to assemble the leg sections and connect them to form the bench frame. Before you screw the horizontal pieces to the legs, pick the best-looking side of the boards and make

Materials list

ITEM	QTY.
2x6 x 8' cedar (rip to 2-1/2" for legs)	1
2x4 x 6' cedar (rip to 2-1/2" for lower cross members)	1
2x4 x 4' cedar	1
1x2 x 4' cedar	3
1x3 x 8' cedar	1
1x4 x 8' cedar	2
1x8 x 4' cedar	3
5/4 x 6 x 4' bullnose cedar	9
2' x 2' 3/4" plywood	1

Hardware

1-1/4" stainless steel screws	80
2" stainless steel screws	50
3" stainless steel screws	10
1-1/4" finish nails	1 lb.
3/8" wood screw plugs*	30
3/8" wood buttons*	10
10-oz. tube of construction adhesive	1
Water-resistant wood glue	1
6" x 8" decorative shelf brackets	4
10" x 14" x 18"-deep wastebasket	1
14" x 20" x 4"-deep litter pan	1
100-grit sandpaper sheets	2

* Wood plugs and buttons are available from home centers and woodworking stores.

1 Mark the notch locations on the legs (A and B) using the dimensions in Figure A. Make a series of 3/4-in.-deep saw kerfs about 1/4 in. apart to create the notches.

Choosing lumber

Make sure to pick straight boards with at least one nice-looking side. You can hide a few minor defects on the back or underside of the bench. Also, avoid boards with large knots, which will weaken key parts and make it harder to cut the notches.

When you get your materials home, cut the pieces to size using the Cutting list p. 116. Many of the parts, like the 1 x 1-in. slats for the grate and the 2-1/2-in.-wide legs, have to be cut the length of the board. This operation, called ripping, is possible with a circular saw, but it's much quicker, easier and more accurate with a table saw.

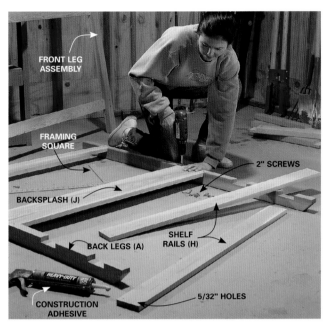

CHISEL

NOTCHES FOR SHELF RAILS (H)

WOOD RASP

FRONT LEG ASSEMBLY

FRAMING SQUARE

BACKSPLASH (J)

2" SCREWS

BACK LEGS (A)

SHELF RAILS (H)

5/32" HOLES

CONSTRUCTION ADHESIVE

2 Chisel out the waste wood from the notches and smooth the bottom with a wood rasp.

3 Spread a small bead of construction adhesive in each notch and lay the horizontal pieces in place. Use a framing square to make sure the cross members are at right angles to the legs, then drive a pair of 2-in. screws at each joint.

sure it's facing the front of the bench. (The best sides are facing down in Photo 3.) Drill 5/32-in. clearance holes through the cross members to avoid splitting them and to allow the screws to draw the boards tight to the legs.

Use only one 1-1/4-in. screw to attach parts F and G to the front legs. Center the screw so it doesn't interfere with the 3-in. screws you'll be installing to secure the leg assembly (Photo 4). Use a 3/4-in. spacer block (Photo 4) to align the cross members (E) before you drive in the 3-in. screws.

If you'll be leaving your bench outdoors, use stainless steel screws or corrosion-resistant deck screws. For extra strength and durability, put a small dab of construction adhesive on each joint before you screw the pieces together. To hide the 3-in. screws that secure the front legs, use a 3/8-in. brad point drill bit to drill 1/4-in.-deep recesses before you drill the 5/32-in. clearance holes. Then glue 3/8-in. wood buttons into the recesses after you screw the parts together.

Keep a framing square handy as you assemble the leg sections and bench frame and use it to make sure the assemblies are square before you tighten the screws.

Photo 5 shows how to mark and cut the plywood that supports the potting soil container. Shown is a plastic wastebasket, but any container with a lip will work. Trace the shape on a piece of plywood and then cut the hole a little smaller so the plywood supports the lip.

The bench top is made of 1-in.-thick bullnose cedar decking. Join two pieces with cleats to make a removable cover for the dirt catcher (Photo 7). Glue 1 x 1-in. slats together with water-resistant wood glue to form the grate (Photo 6). Scrape off excess glue before it dries. Then allow the glue to dry overnight before you sand the grate and trim the ends flush.

Cutting list

KEY	QTY.	SIZE & DESCRIPTION
A	2	1-1/2" x 2-1/2" x 62" (back legs)
B	2	1-1/2" x 2-1/2" x 33" (front legs)
C	2	1-1/2" x 2-1/2" x 21" (lower cross members)
D	1	1-1/2" x 2-1/2" x 21" (middle cross member)
E	2	1-1/2" x 3-1/2" x 21" (upper cross members)
F	2	3/4" x 2-1/2" x 47" (lower rails)
G	1	3/4" x 3-1/2" x 47" (upper rail)
H	2	3/4" x 3-1/2" x 47" (shelf rails)
J	1	3/4" x 7-1/4" x 47" (backsplash)
K	2	3/4" x 7-1/4" x 47" (shelves)
L	1	3/4" x 3-1/2" x 42-1/2" (bench-top support)
M	2	3/4" x 1-1/2" x 10-1/2" (cover cleats)
N	2	3/4" x 1-1/2" x 12-1/2" (grate cleats)
P	2	1" x 5-1/2" x 23" (bench-top ends; cut to fit)
Q	5	1" x 5-1/2" x 23" (bench top)
R	7	1" x 1" x 23-1/2" (slats)
S	12	1" x 1" x 4" (spacers)
T	2	3/4" x 1-1/2" x 25-1/2" (container cleats)
U	2	3/4" x 1-1/2" x 16-3/4" (bench-top cleats)
V	4	1" x 5-1/2" x 47" (lower shelf)
W	1	12-3/4" x 20-1/4" x 3/4" plywood (container support)

Screw cleats to the bottom of the grate to keep it positioned and allow easy removal.

The width of the end pieces (P) varies, depending on the dimensions of your decking. To determine the width, first

Figure A
Potting bench

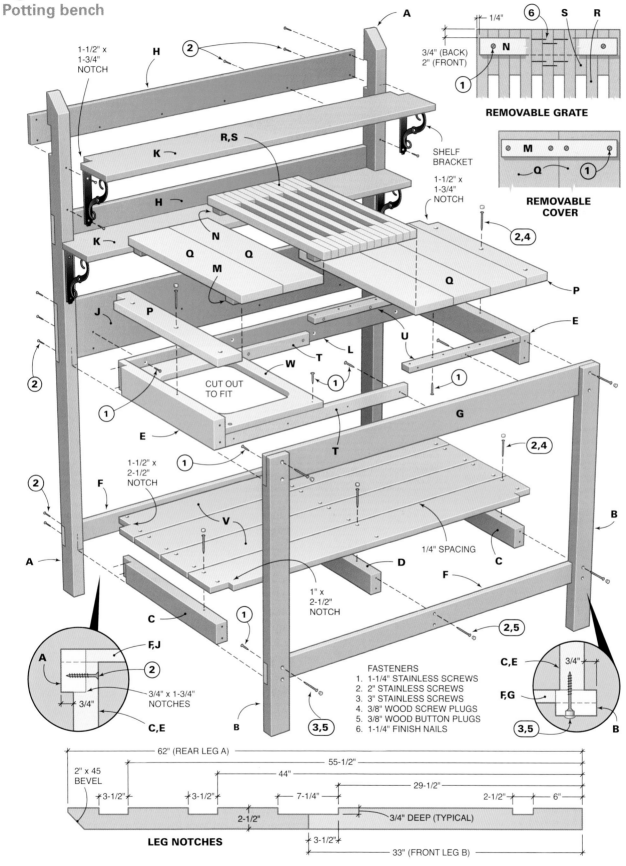

Figure A labels and annotations:

1-1/2" x 1-3/4" NOTCH

H

(2)

A

1/4"

6

S

R

3/4" (BACK)
2" (FRONT)

(1)

N

REMOVABLE GRATE

K

R,S

SHELF BRACKET

H

1-1/2" x 1-3/4" NOTCH

M

(1)

Q

REMOVABLE COVER

K

N

Q

Q

(2,4)

M

Q

P

J

P

E

M

T

L

U

(1)

W

CUT OUT TO FIT

T

(1)

E

G

2

1-1/2" x 2-1/2" NOTCH

F

(1)

(2,4)

A

V

1/4" SPACING

C

2

B

C

F

A

F,J

(2)

3/4" x 1-3/4" NOTCHES

3/4"

C,E

B

1" x 2-1/2" NOTCH

(3,5)

FASTENERS
1. 1-1/4" STAINLESS SCREWS
2. 2" STAINLESS SCREWS
3. 3" STAINLESS SCREWS
4. 3/8" WOOD SCREW PLUGS
5. 3/8" WOOD BUTTON PLUGS
6. 1-1/4" FINISH NAILS

C,E

3/4"

F,G

B

(3,5)

(2,5)

LEG NOTCHES

2" x 45 BEVEL

62" (REAR LEG A)

55-1/2"

44"

29-1/2"

3-1/2"

3-1/2"

7-1/4"

2-1/2"

6"

2-1/2"

3/4" DEEP (TYPICAL)

3-1/2"

33" (FRONT LEG B)

LOWER RAIL (F)

FRONT LEGS (B)

3" SCREWS

3/4" SPACER BLOCK

LOWER CROSS MEMBERS (C)

UPPER CROSS MEMBERS (E)

2" SCREWS

LOWER RAIL (F)

4 Screw the horizontal cross members (C and E) to the back leg assembly. Drill and countersink the front leg assembly and attach it to members C and E with 3-in. screws. Cover the screws with decorative wood buttons.

BENCH-TOP SUPPORT (L)

CONTAINER CLEAT (T)

1/2" STARTER HOLES

JIGSAW

WASTEBASKET OUTLINE

WASTEBASKET

PLYWOOD (W)

5 Trace the wastebasket onto the 3/4-in. plywood (W). Draw a second line about 1/2 in. inside the traced outline. Drill a 1/2-in. starter hole and cut along the inside line with a jigsaw. Screw the bench-top support (L) and container cleats (T) to the bench and screw the plywood (W) into place.

center the grate, removable cover and three more boards on the bench top, leaving an equal space on each end. Then measure the distance from the last board to the outside edge of the back leg and cut and notch the end pieces to fit.

Glue 3/8-in. wood plugs into 3/8-in. by 1/4-in.-deep recesses to hide the screws that hold the two end pieces (P) and lower shelf boards in place. Sand them flush after the glue dries.

Complete the potting bench by notching the 1x8 shelves (Photo 9) and securing them with 2-in. screws through the horizontal 1x4 shelf rails (H).

Protect your bench with a good finish

Unfinished cedar has some resistance to decay, but the best strategy is to apply a top-quality exterior finish to keep the wood from cracking, splitting and rotting. Penetrating oil–type finishes with a small amount of pigment provide a natural look and reduce fading. Finishes that leave a film provide the best protection. Spar varnish or Sikkens are two examples. Take extra precautions to seal the bottom of the legs to keep them from absorbing moisture from the damp ground.

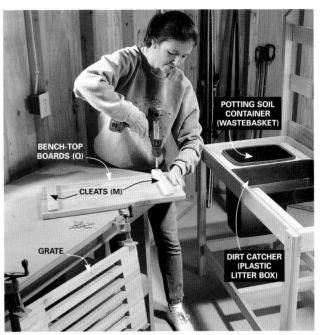

6 Glue and nail the slats and spacers together to make the grate. Drill 1/16-in. pilot holes for the nails to prevent splitting the wood. Spread water-resistant glue on both surfaces and nail the slats and spacers together with 4d galvanized finish nails. Clamp the completed assembly with bar clamps and allow it to dry overnight. Trim the 23-1/2-in. grate to 23 in. with your circular saw or table saw and sand the edge smooth.

7 Assemble the cover for the dirt container by screwing cleats (M) to the bottom of the 5/4 x 6-in. decking (Q). Screw cleats (N) to the bottom of the completed grate.

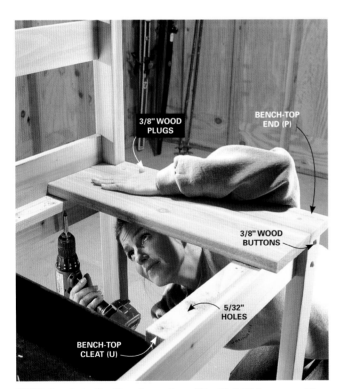

8 Attach the fixed bench-top pieces (Q) with 1-1/4-in. screws driven up through the bench-top cleats (U). Secure the bench-top ends (P) and bottom shelf boards (V) by driving 1-1/4-in. screws through predrilled and countersunk holes. Conceal these screws with wood plugs glued into the recesses. Sand the plugs flush when the glue dries.

9 Notch the shelves (K) and slide them into place. Screw through the shelf rails (H) into the shelves. Support the front of the shelves with metal brackets.

Deluxe drum composter

WHAT IT TAKES

TIME: 1 day
SKILL LEVEL: Intermediate

It's large and loaded with features—but you can build it for the cost of a bargain model

Drum composters convert yard waste to finished compost much faster than stationary compost bins do because they allow you to churn and instantly aerate the waste. Plus, drum composters are easier on your back. You can buy them online or at any garden center in a wide range of sizes and prices. But they all follow the same basic design—a drum on a stand. Our version is an adaptation of that, using a plastic 55-gallon drum. The drum and stand together cost about the same as the low-price models, but our composter is built stronger and has more features. It takes a full day to customize the drum and build the stand. We used rivets to speed up the assembly, but screws, nuts and lock washers work too.

Finding and customizing the drum

Ask for free used 55-gallon polyethylene drums at car washes and food processing and industrial manufacturers. Since beggars can't be choosers, you'll probably wind up with a white, green or blue drum. If that doesn't fit your backyard color scheme (paint doesn't stick well to polyethylene), contact a container firm and order the color you want. We ordered a black "tight-head" drum (top permanently sealed to the drum) from a local supplier.

Next, use a jigsaw to cut a door panel slightly smaller than the width of your wheelbarrow. The next step takes the most time and isn't mandatory, but it adds strength and stability to the entire door assembly: Bend 1/8-in. x 1-in. flat aluminum stock around the drum to form side reinforcements for the door opening. Cut the bent aluminum slightly longer than the door opening and mount it to the drum (Photo 1, p. 123).

Then cut flat aluminum pieces for the top and bottom of the door opening and the hinge side of the door. Mount the top and bottom door opening reinforcements in the same manner. Mount the hinges at the bottom of the door opening so the door hangs down when you empty the drum. Finish the door by adding the latches (Figure A).

To make stirring paddles, cut an 8-ft. piece of 4-in. PVC pipe in half lengthwise using a jigsaw. Cut the halves to length so they're slightly shorter than the inside height of the drum. Arrange two halves back-to-back. Then drill and screw the pieces together to form one paddle unit. The back-to-back design is stronger than a single "scoop" and allows you to rotate the drum in either direction. Repeat for the second paddle unit.

Since the drum has a taper at the top and bottom, you'll have to sand the ends of the paddles to match (Photo 2). Mount the paddle units 180 degrees apart and secure them to the drum with screws, nuts and washers. Finally, mount grab handles around the drum to help you rotate it.

A tight-head drum comes with two threaded "bungholes." Remove the threaded caps to provide ventilation. You may need to drill additional ventilation holes if the mixture stays too wet.

Build the stand and mount the rollers

Cut the legs and deck boards to length according to the Cutting List. Then assemble the stand using a drill and exterior screws (Photo 3). Add diagonal struts to prevent front-to-back and side-to-side movement when spinning the drum.

Flip the stand upright and mount two casters so they ride in the recess around the drumhead. Then level the drum and mount the remaining two casters (Photo 4).

Load, spin and dump

Load the drum with yard waste and add a compost starter to get the batch cooking (sold at any home or garden center). Rotate at least once every day to mix and aerate the batch. When the compost is ready, just dump it out.

How it works

Waste becomes compost thanks to millions of hungry microbes, which break it down and convert it to nutrient-rich fertilizer. Those microbes need oxygen to thrive, and turning the drum daily creates fresh air pockets in the mix. You can accomplish the same thing by churning a pile of compost with a shovel, but a drum composter makes it easier. And the more thorough mixing speeds decomposition.

Rotate daily. Screw the bung caps into the holes to prevent compost from leaking out. Then grab the handles and rotate the drum several times in either direction to stir the mixture.

Drop, roll and dump. Park your wheelbarrow under the drum and open the door. As you roll the drum downward, the compost will dump right into the wheelbarrow.

Figure A Drum composter

Overall dimensions: 39" W x 30" D x 58" H

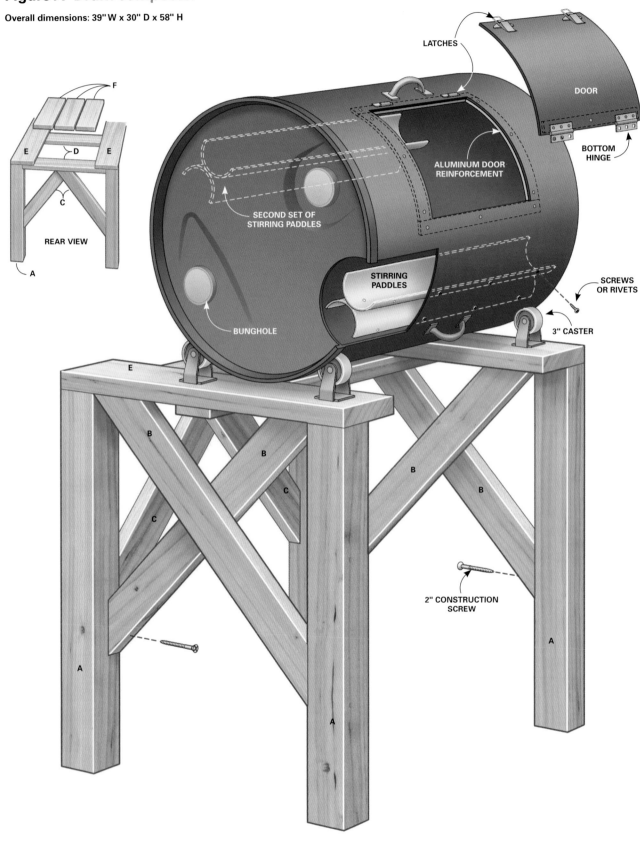

LATCHES

DOOR

BOTTOM HINGE

ALUMINUM DOOR REINFORCEMENT

SECOND SET OF STIRRING PADDLES

F

E   D   E

C

A

REAR VIEW

STIRRING PADDLES

BUNGHOLE

SCREWS OR RIVETS

3" CASTER

E

B

B

B

B

C

C

C

2" CONSTRUCTION SCREW

A

A

A

A

ALUMINUM STRIP

RIVET GUN

1 Reinforce the door opening. Clamp aluminum strips in place so 1/2 in. extends into the door opening. Fasten the strips with rivets or nuts and screws.

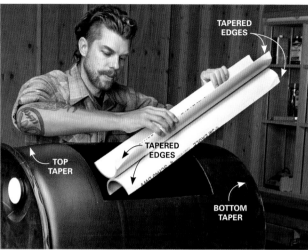

TAPERED EDGES

TAPERED EDGES

TOP TAPER

BOTTOM TAPER

2 Install the paddle. Taper the ends of the paddle to match the tapered ends of the drum. Sand the paddle with a belt sander until it fits. Then install the paddle with screws.

CROSS BRACE

3 Assemble the stand. Screw the legs to the rails. Then install the cross braces. Strengthen with diagonal struts.

PRY BAR

4 Mount the casters. Then set a level on top of the drum and pry the drum up with a board. When the drum is level, position the last caster, mark its location and screw it into place.

Cutting list

KEY.	QTY.	SIZE & DESCRIPTION
A	4	4x4 x 32-1/2" (legs)
B	4	2x4 x 32-3/8" (side braces; cut at 45-degree angle, long point to long point)
C	2	2x4 x 30" (back braces; cut at 45-degree angle, long point to long point)
D	2	2x4 x 32" (cross braces)
E	2	2x8 x 30" (drum deck)
F	3	2x8 x 13-1/2" (deck, evenly spaced; optional)

Materials list

ITEM	QTY.
12' 4x4 treated lumber	1
8' 2x4 treated lumber	3
10' 2x8 treated lumber	1
6' of 4" PVC pipe	

Rivets (aluminum), nuts and bolts (stainless steel), hinges, handles, 1" flat aluminum stock, latches, exterior screws, 3" casters.

9 OUTDOOR TABLES

Faux stone patio table

WHAT IT TAKES

TIME: 1 day, plus a week for drying time

SKILL LEVEL: Intermediate

A different kind of grout

Construction grout is used mostly for heavy construction projects like anchoring steel columns. But it's also perfect for casting projects because it has a creamy consistency that takes on the shape and texture of the form almost perfectly. Use a smooth form and you're guaranteed a smooth, uniform tabletop. Most home centers carry construction grout in 50-lb. bags. (Quikrete Precision Grout and Sakrete Construction Grout are two brands.) Go to quikrete.com or sakrete.com to find a dealer if your store doesn't carry it. Darken the grout by adding cement colorant to the water (Photo 2).

The top is made from construction grout tinted with colorant. Tile grout creates the dark veins.

Build the form

Plastic-coated particleboard (called melamine) is perfect for form work because it's inexpensive and smooth. Cut the form base to 31-1/2 x 31-1/2 in. and then cut 2 x 32-in. strips for the form

Forming a crinkled edge

Smooth edges on the tabletop are fine, but a crinkled edge will give it a more natural look. To start, cut four strips of aluminum foil tape about an inch longer than the form sides. Then...

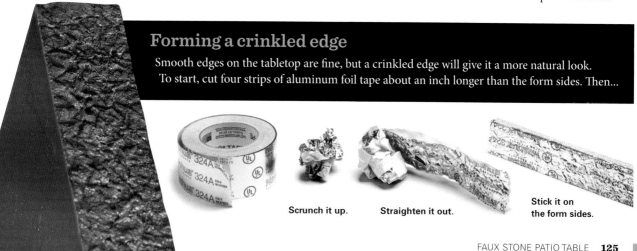

Scrunch it up.   Straighten it out.   Stick it on the form sides.

Figure A Pedestal

The tabletop height is 30 in. The top itself is 30 x 30 in. and 2 in. thick.

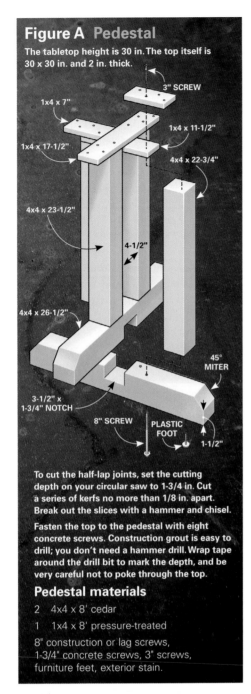

3" SCREW

1x4 x 7"

1x4 x 11-1/2"

1x4 x 17-1/2"

4x4 x 22-3/4"

4x4 x 23-1/2"

4-1/2"

4x4 x 26-1/2"

45° MITER

3-1/2" x 1-3/4" NOTCH

8" SCREW

PLASTIC FOOT

1-1/2"

To cut the half-lap joints, set the cutting depth on your circular saw to 1-3/4 in. Cut a series of kerfs no more than 1/8 in. apart. Break out the slices with a hammer and chisel.

Fasten the top to the pedestal with eight concrete screws. Construction grout is easy to drill; you don't need a hammer drill. Wrap tape around the drill bit to mark the depth, and be very careful not to poke through the top.

Pedestal materials

2   4x4 x 8' cedar

1   1x4 x 8' pressure-treated

8" construction or lag screws, 1-3/4" concrete screws, 3" screws, furniture feet, exterior stain.

Tabletop materials

150 lbs. of construction grout

3/4-in. melamine (sold in 4 x 8-ft. sheets)

Quikrete Cement Color (10 oz.)

Spray lubricant

Plastic cement tub

2-1/2-in.-wide foil tape

2-in. nails or screws

Unsanded tile grout (black or charcoal)

Tile or stone sealer

Welded wire mesh

1 **Build an upside-down form.** Assemble the form, spray on lubricant and wipe off the excess. Cast upside down, the tabletop's surface face will turn out as smooth and flat as the melamine form.

HOMEMADE MEASURING BUCKET

BATCH 1
BATCH 2
BATCH 3

2 **Mix one bag at a time.** Add grout to water mixed with colorant. Turn a bucket into a giant measuring cup so you can easily use the correct amount of colored water with each bag.

3 **Pour a pattern.** Sketch a pattern on the form and fill the outlined areas with mounds of construction grout. This pattern will show up on the top of the table.

sides. Attach the sides to the base as shown in Photo 1. The overhanging sides make dismantling the form easier; you can just whack them loose with a hammer. Coat the form with spray lubricant (Photo 1). Important: Use a lubricant that dries instead of leaving an oily coating. The label will say something like "leaves a dry film."

Next, grab a pencil and sketch a random pattern on the form outlining the areas you'll cover with grout first (Photo 3). The pencil lines will determine where the dark veins appear in the finished top. Set the form on a sturdy work surface

and level the form with shims. Construction grout is slushy and will overflow if the form tilts. Spilled grout will leave stains, so cover the floor with plastic drop cloths.

Get ready to mix

Mixing and pouring the construction grout is a three-phase process: You'll use most or all of the first bag to pour a pattern (Photo 3), the second to fill in the pattern (Photo 6) and the third to completely fill the form.

Turning a bucket into a giant measuring cup (Photo 2) will let you add equal amounts of water and

4 Create the veins. Sprinkle dry tile grout along the edges of the mounds. The colored powder will form dark lines in the finished top.

5 Blow the grout. Turn down the pressure on your compressor and blow the tile grout against the edges of the mounds.

6 Fill in the blank spots. Cover the bare areas of the form. Pour between the areas you covered first, not on top of them. Jiggle the form to spread and level the mix.

7 Add the mesh. With the form about half full, lay in the welded wire mesh for reinforcement. Then completely fill the form.

8 Screed it off. Scrape off the excess using a straight board and a sawing motion. Cover the wet grout with plastic. The longer it stays wet, the stronger it will cure.

9 Seal the tabletop. Bring out the color with sealer. Before you apply the sealer, ease the tabletop's sharp edges with 80-grit sandpaper.

cement colorant to each of the three bags without measuring each time. First, measure the correct amount of water into the bucket (about 4.5 liters per bag) and mark the water level on the bucket. Measure in more water to locate the other two marks (at 9 and 13.5 liters).

Next, empty the bucket and dump in the cement colorant. Much of it will remain in the bottle. To wash it out, pour in a little water, shake hard and pour again. Repeat until all the colorant is washed out. Refill the bucket with water and you'll have tinted water, premeasured into three equal amounts. The colorant tends to settle to the bottom, so stir the colored water before each use.

Construction grout hardens fast. In warm weather, it will become stiff and difficult to work with in just 15 minutes. Minutes wasted cutting the wire mesh or searching for a tool can ruin the project. So have absolutely everything ready to

go before you start mixing. It's best to have a helper, too. To slow down the hardening, use cold water only.

Mix the construction grout in a plastic cement tub. Don't pour the water directly from the bucket into the mixing tub; it's too hard to control the flow. Instead, ladle the water into the tub with a smaller container. Dump in about half the bag and mix it thoroughly. Gradually add the rest of the bag as you mix. If the mixed grout stiffens before you can use it, stir it to restore the slushy consistency. If it becomes too stiff to stir, toss it. The tabletop only requires about 2-1/2 bags, so you can afford to waste some.

Pour, wait patiently and seal

Photos 3 – 9 show how to complete the top. Don't forget to turn down your compressor's pressure to about 5 psi before you blow the tile grout (Photo 5). Cut the 2 x 2-ft. section of mesh (Photo

7) using bolt cutters. Wire cutters won't do the job.

Resist the temptation to tear off the form as soon as the grout is hard. The longer the grout stays wet, the stronger it will get. Give it at least three days. A week is even better. To remove the form, get a helper and flip the form upside down. (Don't let the top tip out of the form!) Then knock the form sides loose with a hammer and lift the form off the top. Don't despair when you unveil the bland, gray top. The sealer will deepen the color and accentuate the black veins (Photo 9). Most sealers can't be applied until the grout has cured for at least 28 days. Before you apply sealer to the top, try it on the underside to make sure you like the look. We used a glossy "stone and tile" sealer to bring out the most color. A sealer with a matte finish will have a subtler look.

Fold-up grill table

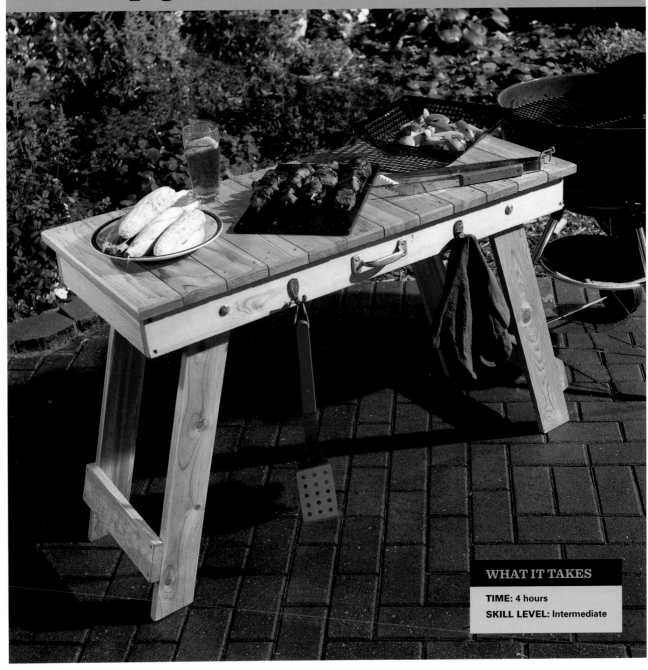

WHAT IT TAKES

TIME: 4 hours
SKILL LEVEL: Intermediate

A handy companion for your barbecue that collapses for easy storage

After building this collapsible cedar table, your family will wonder how they ever grilled without it. The legs nest under the top for quick storage or carrying to all kinds of other jobs, indoors or out. All you need to build it is a drill, a saw, basic hand tools, a short stack of cedar boards and half an afternoon.

The table is made entirely from 1x4 cedar boards. Wood quality varies, so pick over the lumber for flat, straight boards that are free of large or loose knots. You can make the table from eight 6-ft. boards, but buy 10 to allow for possible miscuts and to give you more choice for the top slats.

Figure A
Fold-up grill table

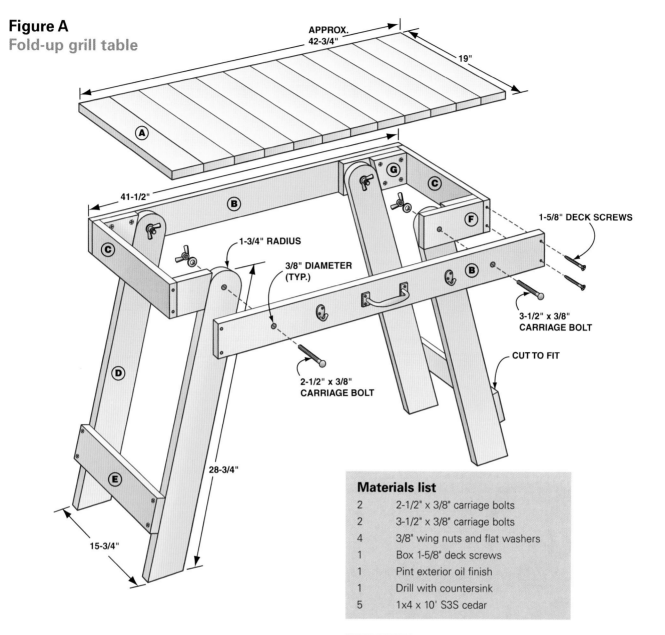

APPROX. 42-3/4"

19"

41-1/2"

1-3/4" RADIUS

3/8" DIAMETER (TYP.)

1-5/8" DECK SCREWS

3-1/2" x 3/8" CARRIAGE BOLT

CUT TO FIT

2-1/2" x 3/8" CARRIAGE BOLT

28-3/4"

15-3/4"

Materials list

2	2-1/2" x 3/8" carriage bolts
2	3-1/2" x 3/8" carriage bolts
4	3/8" wing nuts and flat washers
1	Box 1-5/8" deck screws
1	Pint exterior oil finish
1	Drill with countersink
5	1x4 x 10' S3S cedar

Cut the parts

You can use a handsaw to cut the parts, but a miter saw and jigsaw speed up the job significantly. Use a square to help make straight cuts (Photo 1). To ensure matching legs and frame parts, clamp two boards together and mark and cut them at the same time (Photo 2). Cut slats one or two at a time. You'll cut the stretchers after bolting on the legs.

To assemble the frame, drill two holes in the ends of the longer frame boards and add a countersink hole for the screwheads to nestle into. Cut the slats and place them top-side up on a flat surface (Photo 3). Center the frame on the slats to create a 3/4-in. overhang on all four sides. Then lightly trace the frame shape on the slats with a pencil.

Lift off the frame and drill and countersink screw holes in the slats using the traced lines as a guide. Then screw the slats to the frame (Photo 4). Lightly tap a couple nails between the slats while

Cutting list

Overall Dimensions: 28-1/2"H x 42-3/4"W x 19"D

KEY	NAME	QTY.	DIMENSIONS IN INCHES
A	Top slat	12	1x4 x 19"
B	Long side pc.	2	1x4 x 41-1/2"
C	Short side pc.	2	1x4 x 15-3/4"
D	Leg	4	1x4 x 28-3/4" (15 degree angled end cut)
E	Leg stretchers	2	1x4 x 15-3/4" (Cut to fit)
F	Leg spacers	2	1x4 x 6-3/4"
G	Leg stop blocks	4	1x4 x 4-3/8" (15 degree angled end cut)

Note: All parts cut from "1x4 S3S" cedar, so each board is a "fat" 3/4" thick and 3-1/2" wide, with two smooth edges, one smooth side and one rough side.

1 Cut the boards for the top and the frame that supports it using a jigsaw or handsaw and a square. (See the exploded view diagram on p. 129.)

2 Clamp the leg boards together (rough side in) and cut both of them at once to create identical leg pairs. Drill the 3/8-in. bolt hole in the upper end before unclamping.

FRAME

3/4" OVERHANG

TOP BOARDS

3 Lay the frame on the top boards and lightly trace the frame shape so it's easy to see where to drill holes. Space the top boards with about 1/16-in. gaps between them.

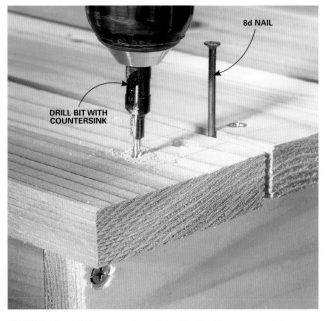

8d NAIL

DRILL BIT WITH COUNTERSINK

4 Drill two holes on each top board end with a countersink bit and screw them to the frame. A nail is handy for creating even spacing.

screwing them to the frame in order to create the approximate 1/16-in. spacing between the slats. The end slats will overhang the frame approximately 3/4 in. to match the slat overhang along the frame sides.

Attach the legs

Flip the tabletop upside down and screw the pair of angled leg stop blocks to the corners of one end (Photo 5). Butt the rounded leg ends against the blocks, then drill and bolt on the outer leg pair with the shorter 2-1/2-in. carriage bolts, washers and wing nuts. Attach the inner leg pair to the other frame, first screwing in the spacer blocks to allow the legs to nest inside the other pair (Photo 6). Add the angled leg stop blocks, then drill and bolt on the second leg pair with the longer 3-1/2-in. carriage bolts.

With the legs flat on the underside of the table, measure for the stretchers, cut, drill and fasten them to the legs (Photo 7). To pull out the legs, lift the more widely spaced pair first so the

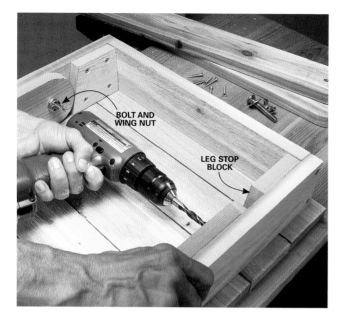

5 Screw a pair of angled leg stop blocks in one end of the frame, then butt the rounded ends of the legs against the blocks. Drill through the frame and bolt on the legs.

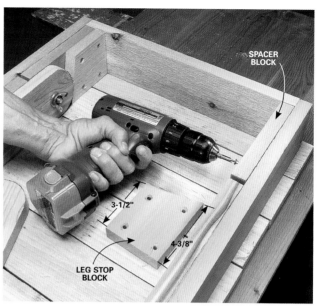

6 Screw spacer blocks in the other frame end. These allow the other pair of legs to nest inside the first pair. Then drill and bolt on the second pair of legs and leg stop blocks.

7 Screw stretchers across each pair of legs. For best fit and overall results, mark and cut the stretchers based on the actual spacing between the legs.

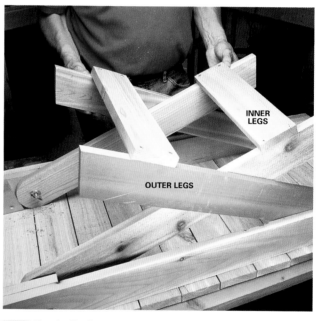

8 Test the fit of the legs in the frame by pulling the legs up from the frame. If they bind and scrape, sand the sides for a smoother fit.

second pair can be raised without catching on the first pair's stretcher (Photo 8).

Sand, finish, then grill

Sand the table with 100-grit paper and, with a sanding block or rasp, slightly round the top edges of the slats. Put on your favorite finish; we used two coats of penetrating oil finish. Pull out the legs, tighten the wing nuts and throw some rib eye steaks on the grill—just in time for dinner!

Stone-top table

The inspiration for this small end table came while browsing through a local tile store, looking at the huge variety of slate, granite, limestone and marble that's available. The table top shown here is 16-in.-square copper slate—a perfect match for the oak base—but many other stone tiles are available.

To make this table, you'll need a power miter saw, drill and hand tools. The stone top doesn't need cutting—just soften the sharp edges with 120-grit sandpaper. The base is made from standard dimension oak, available at home centers. And once you put together the simple cutting and assembly jigs shown in the photos on the next page, the table base almost builds itself.

Figure A
Stone-top table

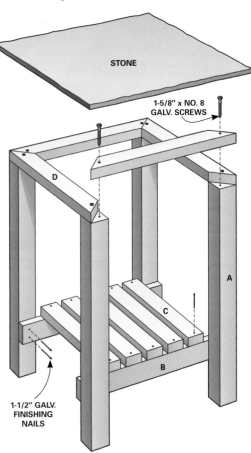

STONE

1-5/8" x NO. 8 GALV. SCREWS

D

A

C

B

1-1/2" GALV. FINISHING NAILS

BLACK SLATE

CREAM QUARTZ

INDIAN AUTUMN SLATE

Materials list

Wood

2	2x2 x 3' oak
14'	1x2 oak

Note: If the table is for outdoor use, use white oak or ash, which are more rot-resistant.

Stone Tile

1	16" x 16" x 1/2"

Hardware

1 lb.	1-1/2" galvanized finishing nails
8	1-5/8" x No. 8 galvanized screws
4	Nylon chair glides
	Exterior wood glue
	Exterior construction adhesive

Cutting list

KEY	NAME	QTY.	DIMENSIONS
A	Leg	4	2x2 x 16-3/4"
B	Shelf supports	2	1x2 x 13-3/4"
C	Shelf slats	5	1x2 x 10-3/4"
D	Mitered top support	4	1x2 x 13-3/4"

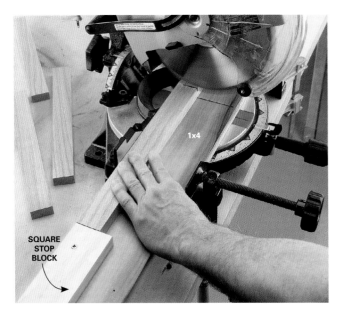

MITERED STOP BLOCK

SQUARE STOP BLOCK

1 Make a jig with square and mitered stop blocks screwed to a straight 1x4. Slide the 1x4 to the right length for each piece and clamp it down. When you cut the miters, set the saw for 45-1/2 degrees. That way, the outside corners of the top—the only part that shows—will be tight even if the top isn't perfectly square. Sand all the oak pieces before beginning assembly.

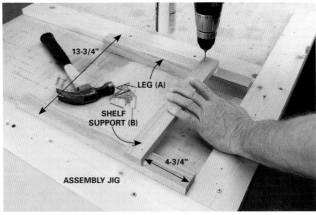

13-3/4"
LEG (A)
SHELF SUPPORT (B)
4-3/4"
ASSEMBLY JIG

2 Set up a square assembly jig with 1x4s attached to your work-bench. Use two shelf supports as spacers to ensure that the jig is the correct width. Set two table legs (A) in the jig and attach a shelf support (B) with glue and nails. Predrill with a 5/64-in. drill bit, or use one of the nails with the head clipped off as the drill bit.

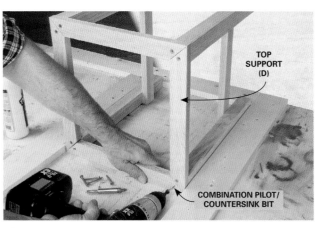

TOP SUPPORT (D)
COMBINATION PILOT/ COUNTERSINK BIT

3 Screw down the mitered top supports (D) with the table still in the jig, using glue and 1-5/8-in. galvanized screws. Predrill and countersink with a combination bit at a slight angle, toward the center of the leg.

SHELF SLAT (C)
LEG (A)
SHELF SUPPORT (B)

4 Predrill and nail the shelf slats with the legs tight and square against the sides of the assembly jig. Attach the center slat first, centering it on the shelf support. Wipe off excess glue and set the remaining slats, using two 1/2-in. spacers. Set the nails, fill the holes, then sand.

CONSTRUCTION ADHESIVE

5 Glue the stone top to the base. First, center the table and trace the top onto the tile. Lay a bead of construction adhesive within the outline, keeping the glue away from the outer edge to avoid oozing. Press the table into the glue. Place a weight on the table for 24 hours until the glue sets. Leave excess glue until it's dry, and then peel it away. Finish the wood with exterior oil or varnish and add a nylon chair glide on the bottom of each leg.

A-frame picnic table

An outdoor dining table you can build in a weekend

WHAT IT TAKES

TIME: 1 weekend
SKILL LEVEL: Intermediate

ere's a great-looking, sturdy picnic table that's strong enough to support eight or more bulky NFL linemen, even after a pregame feast. Plus, it's easy to build and inexpensive because it's made from construction-grade Douglas fir lumber.

This isn't a project that'll take weeks to build. You can buy the lumber, build the table, and apply the finish all in one weekend. You can do it all yourself, but an extra pair of hands comes in handy during assembly.

And it does comfortably seat eight people, even 10, if everyone gets along!

What you need to build it

You'll need a circular saw, belt sander, drill, a 1-in. dia. spade bit, a few drill bits, a ratchet with a 9/16-in. socket to tighten the nuts, a hammer, tape measure, screwdriver, four bar clamps and a pair of sawhorses. If you have a Speed square, use it to guide the circular saw as you cut the ends of the top and seat boards.

The A-frame pieces (B, C and D) are joined with carriage bolts. A carriage bolt doesn't look like a regular bolt. It has a round head with a short, square nub directly under it. You drive it into its hole with a hammer, and the square part locks it into the wood to keep it from turning as you tighten the nut. We used carriage bolts to give the outside ends a more decorative look.

Instead of standard wood screws, use deck screws to prevent rust. The deck screws also have coarse threads for extra grip. To prevent splitting, be sure to drill pilot holes before driving the screws.

Materials list

5	2x10 x 8' construction-grade Douglas fir (or other rot-resistant wood)
2	2x8 x 8' construction-grade Douglas fir
3	2x6 x 8' construction-grade Douglas fir
16	3/8" x 3" galvanized carriage bolts, washers and nylon lock nuts
34	3" deck screws
1 qt.	exterior penetrating clear wood finish and preservative

Figure A
Picnic table details

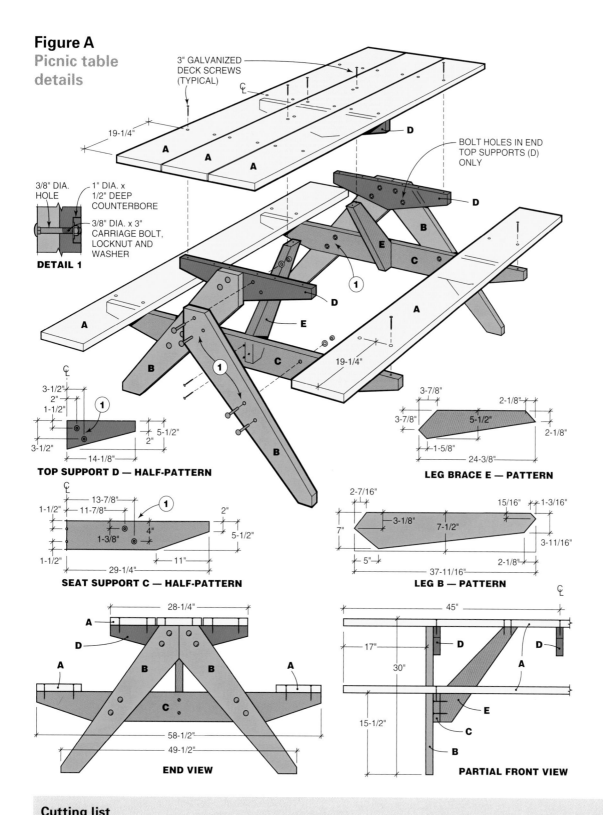

3" GALVANIZED DECK SCREWS (TYPICAL)

19-1/4"

A   A   A

BOLT HOLES IN END TOP SUPPORTS (D) ONLY

D

3/8" DIA. HOLE

1" DIA. x 1/2" DEEP COUNTERBORE

3/8" DIA. x 3" CARRIAGE BOLT, LOCKNUT AND WASHER

DETAIL 1

D

B

E

C

D

A

E

B

19-1/4"

3-1/2"
2"
1-1/2"

5-1/2"
2"

3-1/2"

14-1/8"

TOP SUPPORT D — HALF-PATTERN

3-7/8"
2-1/8"
3-7/8"
5-1/2"
2-1/8"
1-5/8"
24-3/8"

LEG BRACE E — PATTERN

13-7/8"
11-7/8"
1-1/2"
2"
1-3/8"   4"
5-1/2"
1-1/2"
11"
29-1/4"

SEAT SUPPORT C — HALF-PATTERN

2-7/16"
7"
3-1/8"   7-1/2"
15/16"   1-3/16"
3-11/16"
5"   2-1/8"
37-11/16"

LEG B — PATTERN

28-1/4"
A
D
A   B   B   A
C
58-1/2"
49-1/2"

END VIEW

45"
17"   D   D
30"   A
15-1/2"   E
C
B

PARTIAL FRONT VIEW

Cutting list

KEY	QTY.	SIZE & DESCRIPTION
A	5	1-1/2" x 9-1/2" x 90" fir (top and seats)
B	4	1-1/2" x 7-1/2" x 37-11/16" fir (legs)
C	2	1-1/2" x 5-1/2" x 58-1/2" fir (seat supports)

KEY	QTY.	SIZE & DESCRIPTION
D	3	1-1/2" x 5-1/2" x 28-1/4" fir (top supports)*
E	2	1-1/2" x 5-1/2" x 24-3/8" fir (leg braces)

*D length is equal to the total width of the three top pieces (A) plus 1/2 in.

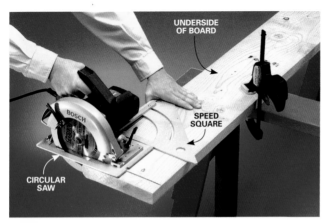

1 Use a circular saw to cut the seat and top boards to length. Try to cut away the checks (cracks) on both ends of the boards. If you have a Speed square, use it to guide the saw as you cut the ends square.

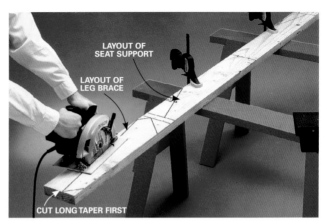

2 Cut the long tapered sides of the leg braces (E) and legs (B) before you cut the pieces to length. This way you can easily clamp the boards to your sawhorses to hold them as you make the cuts.

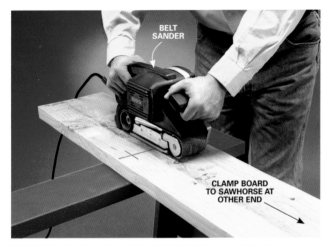

3 Use a belt sander and an 80-grit belt to smooth the boards. To sand board edges, clamp them upright between your sawhorses and sand them with the belt sander or by hand.

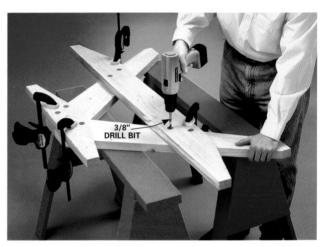

4 Drill the pilot holes for the carriage bolts in the legs. Use the holes drilled in the seat and top supports as drilling guides.

Step-by-step instructions

1. As shown in Photo 1, cut the top and seat pieces (A) to the length given in the Cutting List.
2. Using the dimensions in Figure A, draw the shapes of pieces B through E on your boards. To get the most out of your lumber, place one leg brace (E) and one seat support (C) on one 2x6 board. Put the narrow end of the leg brace at the end of the board. Duplicate this layout on one more 2x6, then draw the three top supports (D) on the remaining 2x6. Also lay out the legs (B) on the 2x8 boards with the narrow ends of the legs at the ends. To make cutting the tapers a bit easier, cut the long sides of the leg braces (E) and legs (B) first, then cut the pieces to length (Photo 2).
3. Drill the holes for the screws and carriage bolts in every part except the legs and leg braces. You'll drill these later during assembly.
4. Use a belt sander with an 80-grit belt to smooth all of the surfaces (Photo 3). Then finish any sharp edges by hand, sanding with 80-grit sandpaper.

5. Now make the A-frame assembly from parts B, C and D. Align the top edge of the seat support (C) 15-1/2 in. up from the bottoms of the legs (B), and center it. Then align the top support (D) parallel to the seat support, and centered as well. Now, drill the carriage bolt holes through the legs using the counterbored holes in the seat support and top support as drilling guides (Photo 4).
6. Keeping each A-frame assembly clamped, flip the end over and hammer in the carriage bolts (Photo 5).
7. Flip the assembly again and put on the washers and nuts. Tighten them with a ratchet and 9/16-in. socket (Photo 6).
8. Align and screw the outside top pieces (A) to the top supports (Photo 7).

Tip

When cutting with a circular saw, cut with the underside of the board facing up. This will help eliminate nasty-looking edges.

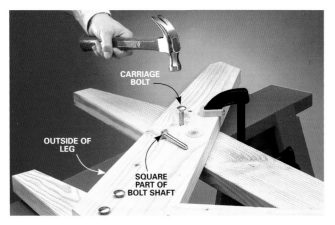

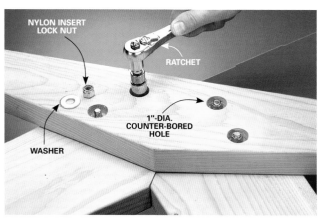

5 Hammer the carriage bolts into their holes. Insert them all the way to "seat" the square part of the bolt shafts securely in the wood.

6 Tighten the nuts with a ratchet and socket. Use nylon insert lock nuts to eliminate lock washers.

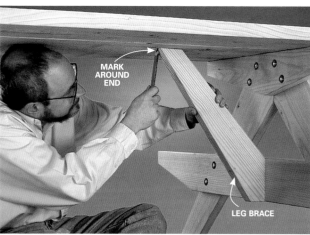

7 Screw the outside top boards to the top supports. Hold the assembled ends upright by placing bar clamps at the bottoms of the legs.

8 Align and mark the spot where the leg braces (E) land on the center top board. If you're working alone, you can do it from underneath.

9. Align and screw the center top board (A) so the gaps between all the boards are equal. Square the top of the table by measuring the diagonal dimensions of the top until they're equal.

10. A helper can make this step easier. Flip the table over and align the leg braces (E) with the top as shown in Figure A. Drill pilot holes, then screw the leg braces to the seat supports and center top board.

11. Align and screw the center top support (D) in place, then attach the seat boards (A).

12. Before applying the finish, unscrew the seat boards and the outside top boards. Removing just these pieces lets you get into tight corners without taking apart the whole table.

13. Apply the finish in a shaded area using the directions given on the can of clear wood preservative finish. Use a 3-in. disposable foam roller to apply the finish on the large surfaces, and a brush for the tight areas.

14. Let the finish dry for two days, then reattach the seat boards and top boards, and you're ready to picnic!

Using construction-grade lumber

Construction-grade lumber is milled for use in home construction. It has lots of knots, cracks and other defects. You can use it to build this table and other outdoor furniture, if you're cautious.

Look for straight, flat boards with no loose knots. Inspect the edges and ends for defects and cracks. Look for bad edges that may turn into nasty splinters later. If you're stuck with bad edges, hide them underneath and on the insides of the seat and top boards.

Finding boards with no end checks is nearly impossible. The table is 90 in. long so you could cut off a total of 6 in. from the checked ends. Don't worry about minor surface roughness; you can sand the wood smooth with a belt sander.

If you plan to buy your wood a few days before you start, store it in a shaded area. When you build the table, pick a shaded area so the sun doesn't dry the wood too fast and cause more cracking.

10 QUICK PROJECTS

WHAT IT TAKES

TIME: All the projects in this chapter can be built in half a day or less.
SKILL LEVEL: Beginner

Mud-busting boot scraper

Ordinary doormats simply can't handle serious muck, but you can clean out packed dirt from even the deepest boot treads with this boot scraper made from 2x4s.

1. Screw the base pieces (A and B) together upside down so that the screw heads are hidden.
2. Fasten the uprights (C) to the sides (D), then screw the side brushes on with 2-in. screws.
3. Screw the bottom brushes to the base with 2-in. screws.
4. Space the side pieces so that the bristles are roughly 4-1/2 in. apart.
5. Add a piece of aluminum angle to the front edge so you can scrape boots before brushing them.

Use stiff-bristle brushes—either "bilevel" brushes or deck scrub brushes. You may need to cut off part of the handle so the brush will lie flat.

Figure A
Boot scraper

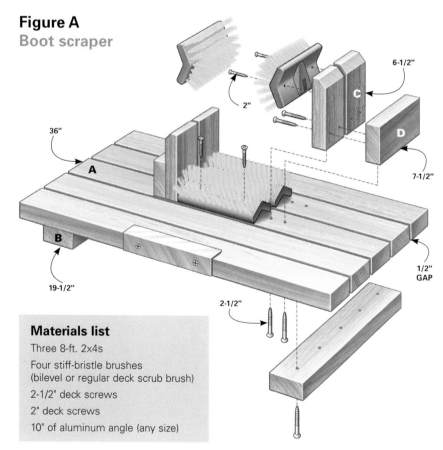

Materials list
Three 8-ft. 2x4s

Four stiff-bristle brushes
(bilevel or regular deck scrub brush)

2-1/2" deck screws

2" deck screws

10" of aluminum angle (any size)

Quick workbench for outdoor projects

FIVE-MINUTE WORKBENCH

CARRYING HANDLE

SHELF

Build a five-minute workbench

You can set up a semipermanent workstation with sawhorses when you're working outside. Screw 2x4s to the tops of the sawhorses and a plywood platform to the 2x4s and you're ready to build. Let the 2x4s project a few inches beyond the plywood to make it easier for someone to help you pick up the whole works and move it around as needed. To keep the clutter out from underfoot, install a temporary plywood shelf across the braces.

Compost sifter

Sifting compost through a coarse screen of 1/4-in. hardware cloth removes sticks and other large chunks, and leaves you with a wheelbarrow full of rich, fluffy compost. Return the large stuff to the compost pile, where it will continue to break down. Size the sifter to fit over your wheelbarrow or just prop one end up and sift right onto the ground.

You'll need about 10 ft. of 1x6 lumber for the sides and another 10 ft. of 1x2 to clamp the screen to the bottom for the bottom screen molding. The lumber species doesn't matter, but cedar will last longer than untreated pine. Buy a 24-in. x 36-in. piece of 1/4-in. hardware cloth and cut it with tin snips to cover the bottom of the completed frame.

OVERHANG PROTECTS AGAINST SHARP SCREEN

1x2

1/4" HARDWARE CLOTH

1/4" HARDWARE CLOTH

1x6

Cut two 36-in. lengths and two 22-1/2 in. lengths of 1x6 pine. Drill 5/32-in. clearance holes 3/8 in. from the ends of the 36-in. boards and screw the corners together with 2-in. deck screws to form the sifter frame. Cut a piece of 1/4-in. hardware cloth to fit and staple it to the bottom of the box. Cut two 37-in. pieces and two 22-in. pieces of 1x2. Drill clearance holes and screw them to the bottom. Overhang the 1x2s 1/2 in. to cover any sharp edges of screen that may be sticking out.

2" GALVANIZED DECK SCREWS

1x2

STAPLER

TIN SNIPS

Build a rain barrel

Install a large valve to quickly fill watering cans and a smaller valve for a garden hose. Secure the valves to the cross brace with J-brackets.

Rain barrels are expensive, but it's pretty easy to build your own from plastic drums or trash cans. Check online for an "open head" plastic 55-gallon drum with a cover. Or find a used barrel by talking to car wash managers (they buy soap and wax by the barrel). If you can't find a container you like, buy a large, heavy-duty garbage can at a home center. All the other materials will be available there too.

Place the drum near a downspout, drill a hole in the side near the bottom and screw in a drain valve. That's an OK installation if you plan to run a soaker hose to your garden. But if you want to use a wand or a spray nozzle, you'll need to elevate the barrel on a stand for more water pressure. Water is heavy (55 gallons weighs 440 lbs.), so use 4x4 treated lumber for the legs and secure everything with construction screws or stainless steel lags. But don't place the stand on soft ground. You could kill somebody if the rig toppled over. If

Figure A Trash can rain barrels

You can make cheap, functional rain barrels with trash cans and simple PVC plumbing and electrical conduit fittings. Line up as many as you need to meet your watering needs.

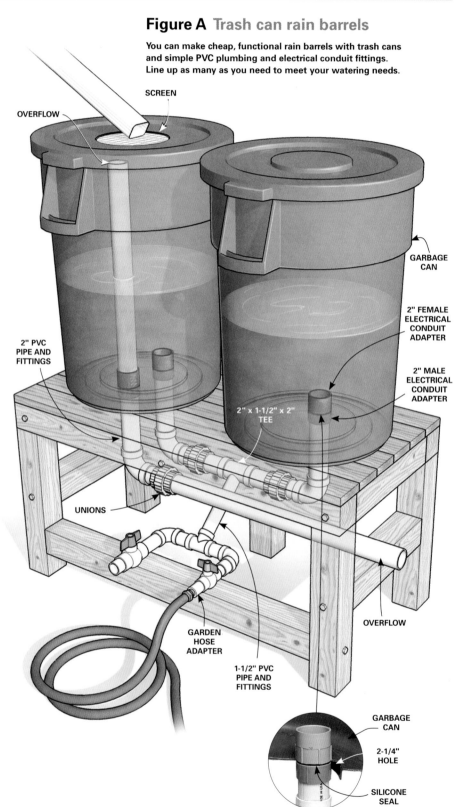

SCREEN

OVERFLOW

GARBAGE CAN

2" FEMALE ELECTRICAL CONDUIT ADAPTER

2" MALE ELECTRICAL CONDUIT ADAPTER

2" PVC PIPE AND FITTINGS

2" x 1-1/2" x 2" TEE

UNIONS

OVERFLOW

GARDEN HOSE ADAPTER

1-1/2" PVC PIPE AND FITTINGS

GARBAGE CAN

2-1/4" HOLE

SILICONE SEAL

you have large gardens and want to store more water, double-size the stand and add a second barrel.

Cut holes in the bottoms of the barrels with a 2-1/4-in. hole saw. Then screw in a 2-in. male threaded electrical (gray PVC) conduit adapter (electrical adapters aren't tapered like plumbing adapters, so you can tighten them down all the way). Squirt a thin bead of silicone caulk around the opening and screw on a threaded electrical PVC coupler to cinch the barrel between the two fittings (Figure A). Next, glue together sections of 2-in. PVC pipe, unions (to make winter disassembly easier), reducers and valves. As long as you're at it, install an overflow pipe so you can direct the excess where you want it.

Finally, cut a hole in one of the covers and mount a screen to filter out leaves and debris. Then just wait for the next big rain.

Rock dolly

Big-foot shoe cleaner

Don't give grass clippings and sawdust a free pass indoors. Screw a stiff brush to a hunk of plywood and give grass and gunk the brush-off before they enter your home.

STIFF BRUSH

BIG PLYWOOD FOOT

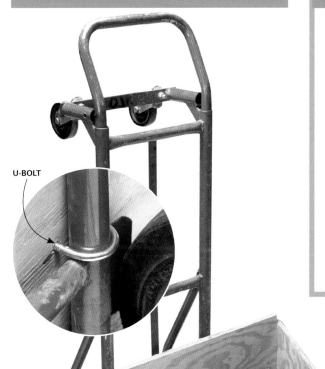

U-BOLT

Need to move stones, potted trees or bags of soil? Make your own sturdy garden dolly from a two-wheel hand truck and plywood. You can make the box any size you want (a box 31 in. wide will still fit through a doorway) and then attach it to your hand truck with U-bolts. It can handle a lot of weight and is easily removed. It's also low to the ground, so you can just roll stones and other heavy items right into it without lifting.

Grow your own 2x4s

Caution: A few days before you dig, call 811 to have your underground utilities marked.

Don't add soil amendments

For years, experts recommended adding compost, peat moss or fertilizer to the planting hole. However, most now agree that you shouldn't backfill with anything other than the original soil from the planting hole. Soil amendments in the planting hole can discourage the tree roots from spreading into the surrounding soil and can cause poor water drainage. Also, in some instances, fertilizers can kill young roots.

Plant in fall or early spring

The ideal time to plant a tree is in early spring before "bud break" or in the fall before the tree goes dormant. Cool weather allows the tree to establish roots in its new location before new top growth puts too much demand on it. Some trees establish better if planted in early spring. These include oaks, pines, dogwoods, American holly, willows and black gum. Avoid planting trees during the summer when they're in full leaf and susceptible to heat stress.

Dig a shallow, broad hole

Dig a saucer-shape hole three to five times the diameter of the root-ball (or the spread of the roots for a bare-root tree). This allows the roots to easily penetrate the softened backfill and properly anchor the tree.

If you're planting in clay or wet soil, use a garden fork or your spade to roughen the bottom and sides of the planting hole to avoid "glazing." Glazing happens when the sides and bottom of a hole become so smooth and compacted that water can't pass easily through the soil. In extreme situations, it could block roots from penetrating the sides of the planting hole.

Don't plant too deep

If you plant the root-ball of a tree too deep, new roots can girdle the trunk and may also suffer from a lack of oxygen. Plant a tree so the root collar—where the uppermost roots attach to the trunk—is about an inch above the soil level.

In many cases, containerized trees from nurseries are planted too deep. Don't go by the soil level in the container. Dig down into the planting medium to find the root collar so you know how deep to plant the tree.

If you're planting a bare-root tree, leave a cone of soil at the bottom of the planting hole and set the root system on top. Place the handle of your shovel flat across the hole from one side to the other to make sure the crown is level with the surrounding soil. You should be able to partially see the root collar, or trunk flare, after the tree is planted.